ANGER MANAGEMENT FOR PARENTS SIMPLIFIED

THE 3-STEP SYSTEM TO CALM YOUR ANGRY
OUTBURSTS, SOOTHE STRESS AND MANAGE ANXIETY
TO IMPROVE YOUR COMMUNICATION AND BOND
WITH YOUR CHILD

CHRISTINE PRATT

Serenity
Parenting

Copyright © 2023 Pratt Publishing LLC. All rights reserved.

The content contained within this book may not be reproduced, duplicated or transmitted without direct written permission from the author or the publisher.

Under no circumstances will any blame or legal responsibility be held against the publisher, or author, for any damages, reparation, or monetary loss due to the information contained within this book.

Either directly or indirectly. You are responsible for your own choices, actions, and results.

Legal Notice:

This book is copyright protected. This book is only for personal use. You cannot amend, distribute, sell, use, quote or paraphrase any part, or the content within this book, without the consent of the author or publisher.

Disclaimer:

Please note the information contained within this document is for educational and entertainment purposes only. All effort has been executed to present accurate, up to date, and reliable, complete information. No warranties of any kind are declared or implied.

Readers acknowledge that the author is not engaging in the rendering of legal, financial, medical or professional advice. The content within this book has been derived from various sources. Please consult a licensed professional before attempting any techniques outlined in this book.

Do not disregard professional medical advice or delay seeking it because of information you have read in this book. If you believe you may be suffering from any medical condition, you should seek immediate medical attention. The use of the advice contained within this book is at the sole discretion of the reader.

By reading this document, the reader agrees that under no circumstances is the author responsible for any losses, direct or indirect, which are incurred as a result of the use of the information contained within this document, including, but not limited to errors, omissions, or inaccuracies.

Brand Design by Kata Kane (kata-kane.com)

Editing by Rose Roman (linkedin.com/in/rose-roman-72381016b)

Interior Book Design by Publishing Services

Published in the United States of America

SOCIAL MEDIA PAGES

Are you ready to evolve into a serene, empowered parent? By cultivating our own inner peace and well-being, let's confidently nurture and shape our children, our future leaders of tomorrow.

Follow **Serenity Parenting** on social media to unlock tips and insights that will guide you on this journey.

And don't just follow — engage with us! Share your stories, seek advice, and be part of a community dedicated to mindful parenting. Together, let's mold a brighter future, one nurturing moment at a time.

Your journey towards peaceful, empowered parenting starts here!

FREE SPECIAL BONUS!

Thank you for choosing our book on your path to mastering anger management! To express our gratitude and support you even further, we're thrilled to present an exclusive gift - a set of Calming Exercises, absolutely FREE with your purchase!

These exercises are specially designed to be quick, easy, and effective, seamlessly integrating into your busy life. Whether you have just a few minutes a day or more, these techniques are tailored to help you maintain your cool, no matter the situation.

https://prattpublishingllc.ac-page.com/free-calming-exercises-guidebook

Scan this QR code to claim your free Calming Exercises:

Embrace this opportunity to transform your approach to anger management. Claim your free Calming Exercises, and start your journey to a more serene you today!

https://prattpublishingllc.ac-page.com/free-calming-exercises-guidebook

CONTENTS

Introduction — 11

STEP 1: ACKNOWLEDGE YOU ARE BEING TRIGGERED

1. UNDERSTANDING ANGER — 19
   Misconceptions About Anger — 20
   Emotional Response Cycle: Why Anger Occurs — 21
   Different Kinds of Anger — 22
   Dealing with Anger — 23
   Understanding How Anger Affects Your Health — 25
   How Anger Affects Relationships — 26
   Things to Watch Out For — 28
   What Healthy Anger Expression Looks Like — 29

2. DISCIPLINE WITH A SMILE — 33
   The Importance of Positive Reinforcement and Praise — 33
   Strategies for Effective Discipline Without Anger — 37
   Managing Anger in Challenging Situations — 40
   Setting and Maintaining Boundaries in a Positive Way — 43
   Checklist to Help You Stop Yelling at Your Kids — 45

3. NAVIGATING PARENTING TRIGGERS — 47
   What Not to Do When Anger Strikes — 48
   The Downfalls of "Old-School" Punishment — 50
   Practical Techniques for Disarming Your Triggers — 52
   Coping Strategies When Anger is Unavoidable — 55
   Are You an Effective Parent? — 57

STEP 2: DISENGAGE AND DEFUSE THE SITUATION

4. THE POWER OF STEPPING AWAY — 61
   Stepping Away from Anger — 62
   Choosing the Higher Ground: Walking Away from a Fight — 65
   Practicing Emotional Regulation & Recentering — 67

5. FINDING AND UNDERSTANDING YOUR CALM — 73
   Importance of Mindfulness and Being Present — 74
   Strategies for Centering Yourself — 78
   Calming Activity Bingo Sheet — 83

6. EFFECTIVE STRATEGIES FOR ANGER PREVENTION — 87
   Exploring the Link Between Stress and Anger in Parenting — 88
   The Impact of Self-Care on Anger Management — 92
   Self-Care Worksheet — 96

STEP 3: RE-ENGAGE WITH YOUR CHILD

7. STRENGTHENING BONDS AND RECONNECTING WITH YOUR CHILD — 105
   Discussing Anger and Finding Solutions Together — 106
   Reconnecting with Your Child After a Conflict — 109
   Importance of Effective Communication in Anger Management — 111
   Strategies for Active Listening and Assertive Expression — 113
   Managing Conflict in a Healthy Way — 115
   Active Listening and Conflict Resolution Worksheet — 117

8. SPEAK THEIR LANGUAGE:
   COMMUNICATION SKILLS FOR EVERY AGE   119
   Communication Examples for Babies and
   Toddlers   121
   Communication Examples for Young Children   124
   Communication Examples for Pre-Teens   127
   Communication Examples for Teenagers   130
   Communication Worksheet   132

9. BUILDING RESILIENCE AND COPING
   SKILLS FOR LIFE   135
   Strategies for Building Resilience in Parents
   and Children   136
   Maintaining Progress and Long-Term Anger
   Management   141
   Staying Motivated and Avoiding Relapse   142
   Resiliency Worksheet   144

   Conclusion   149
   References   153

INTRODUCTION

No one expects parenting to be a breeze, but did you know that more than half of the parents in the United States underestimate the difficulty of parenting? According to the PEW Research Center, 36% of surveyed parents think "being a parent has been somewhat harder compared with how they thought parenting would be." Another 26% of parents think it's "a lot harder" than expected.

Yikes! With so many parents in over their heads, it comes as no surprise that some of them find it challenging to manage their anger. If you're one of these parents, know that you're not alone. Other parents have that same short fuse on certain days. You know, *those* days. Like when the kids decide to wash the dog in the middle of the living room. Or use the fridge as a canvas for fingerpainting. Or refuse to wash the dishes or clean their rooms.

That anger doesn't feel good, does it? You may even feel ashamed of your reactions sometimes. I get it. In fact, that guilt is probably why you turned to this book. You may already notice that your anger is causing problems, and you want to stop them from getting worse. Your home isn't the happy, tranquil environment it used to be because of all the fighting. Because of this turbulence, you and your child are drifting apart.

I'm here to tell you that you can relax!

That's right. You still have time to become the parent you've always wanted to be. In this book, I'll show you how you can transform into that smiling, cheerful parent you thought you'd be. You know that irritatingly perky mom in the PTA who doesn't get phased by anything? That could be you!

This is all possible through my three-step system for managing anger. There are just three simple things you need to do when you're facing one of those tricky situations: **acknowledge** the situation, **disengage** from it, and **re-engage** when you're ready.

My book breaks down each step into three chapters. Each chapter offers plenty of science-backed tips for navigating the anger management process. After reading this book, you'll walk away with:

- **An in-depth understanding of anger:** You'll get a better idea of what you're reacting to, how you're responding to that trigger, and why. I'll cover the ins and outs of anger in general, including the different types. And trust me, there are lots!
- **Practical anger management techniques:** As you read, you'll pick up some real-life techniques to keep your anger in check. I'm here to give you specifics on what you can do and say as you rebuild your

relationship with your child. These are practical, effective, and science-backed methods.
- **Improved communication skills:** My book will also provide alternative ways to get your child's attention without shouting. That's right. You can have a healthy, even fun, discussion with your kid about what to do and what not to do.
- **Guilt management and self-compassion:** We've all done things we're not proud of. Whether it's the smaller things in life, like experimenting with a perm we had no business trying, or the larger ones – like telling your kid they're wreaking havoc on your life. But know this: Acknowledging and dealing with that guilt will help you move on and rebuild your confidence in your parenting skills. I'll show you how.
- **Healthier family environment:** This book can also help you transform your family dynamic from one of chaos to one of tranquility. No, we're not talking about turning you into the mom from *The Brady Bunch* (I promise, no mullet is required!). I'm talking about learning to model respectful behavior for your children so that they can treat you and other family members with the same care and love. (Okay, so it might be a little Brady Bunchy, but hey, that's not *so* bad, right?)

Keep in mind that unlearning those bad habits you've collected over time doesn't happen overnight. In the same vein, learning effective, appropriate anger management habits takes time, too. It will likely take you only a couple of hours to read this book, but it will take a bit more work on your end to make these techniques stick. In other words, you'll need to devote time to implementing the skills you've read about.

But don't worry. I promise you, your parenting life will get better once you've mastered those three basic steps (acknowledge, disengage, and re-engage). I'm going to mention these steps a lot throughout each chapter because I truly believe they are the key to peaceful parenting. Gone are the days when parents thought spanking was the end-all approach to parenting (News flash: The American Academy of Pediatrics states that spanking is harmful to children and ineffective.)

Does practicing these three steps mean you'll never get angry at your child? Absolutely not. That sweet angel of yours will still get under your skin from time to time. But it does mean that you'll have the tools to manage that anger when it appears. Those tools will keep you from saying and doing things you later regret. They'll help you show your child what a responsible, calm parent looks like.

Remember that it has taken me years to learn these strategies for dealing with little ones and managing my anger. There's been a lot of trial and error along the way. I hope this book saves you the trouble of going through what I've been through!

When you're inevitably facing challenges, take a moment to envision what life will be like once you learn to rein in your anger. Those situations that used to end in explosive outbursts will actually play out calmly. If your child starts to throw things because they want to watch one last episode of

Paw Patrol, you can peacefully redirect your child instead of flying off the handle.

Does it sound too good to be true? It really isn't.

Investing in anger management techniques now will save you (and your child) pain down the road. Trust me. There are few quicker ways to ensure an estranged parent-child relationship than to fill your kid's childhood with yelling, belittling, and corporal punishment.

I know you love your child, and you know you love your child. Now let's make it easier for *your child* to know you love them.

STEP 1: ACKNOWLEDGE YOU ARE BEING TRIGGERED

1

UNDERSTANDING ANGER

"Holding on to anger is like grasping a hot coal with the intent of throwing it at someone else; you are the one who gets burned."

— BUDDHA

"Life with my child is exactly how I imagined!" ... said no one ever. Let's face it. Before you welcomed your child into your life, you probably had an Instagram-fueled vision of parenthood. Maybe that image included playing baseball in the backyard or helping your kid design prize-winning science-fair projects.

But if you've picked up this book, your current parenting experience has probably strayed far from those idyllic scenes. Those baseball sessions may be more akin to shouting matches because your child hit the ball into your windshield (even though you told them FIVE times to watch out for it.) Maybe that science fair project turned out iffy because they didn't tell you about the assignment until thirty minutes before bedtime — the night before it was due.

And, again, if you're reading this book, you're probably not happy with how you react to these types of parenting situations. You're a ball of anger, basically. And this anger is starting to affect your relationship with your child.

Luckily, you don't have to spend the next few decades in a constant rage. Like with most changes people make, the first step is recognizing that there's an issue. You must accept that **you have an anger management problem.** Does this mean you're a terrible parent? No. Does it mean you're doomed to become your crabby dad that you can only stand to be around on holidays? Not at all. Put those feelings of shame on the back burner and take a deep breath. You are officially on the road to anger management! Once you've harnessed that fiery, angry inner self, you'll be able to communicate with your kids like Mr. Rogers himself.

MISCONCEPTIONS ABOUT ANGER

Before we dive into what anger is, let's discuss what anger *isn't*. Plenty of myths exist about anger, and getting rid of those misconceptions right away makes managing your anger so much easier.

First off, anger is not an appropriate way to stand up for yourself. Trust me. No one believes for a second you're the one in charge when you're screaming at your kid. Not even your kid. When your face turns red from anger and you wave your hands around frantically, you look exactly how you feel: out of control. There are other, more effective ways to make yourself heard.

A second misconception is that some situations will make anyone angry. While it's true that everyone has triggers, that doesn't mean everyone reacts the same way to the same situation. Believe it or not, some parents have evolved to laugh when their toddler throws spaghetti on the kitchen walls or does their best Picasso impression with a Sharpie on the new (and expensive) windows.

A third thing people mistakenly believe is that some people are naturally angry, and there's no hope for them. Sure, it may feel like you are an irrevocably angry parent, but thankfully, that's just not true. There are tons of resources out there to help, but you must be willing to use them. Reading this book is a great first step!

EMOTIONAL RESPONSE CYCLE: WHY ANGER OCCURS

Now, let's get into what anger *is*. Like other emotions, anger is a reaction to internal or external factors. Something (an "event") happens, your brain processes that event, and anger results. Then, you either manage the anger internally or express it externally.

Consider the following scenario.

The event: You ask your five-year-old to clean up their toys and get ready for bed. Your child refuses and keeps playing.

The processing: Your brain processes that your child is refusing to do what you've asked.

The emotional response: You begin to feel rage at their refusal.

The reaction: You then yell at your kid, telling them they can forget about going to the park the next day.

This example illustrates a typical external anger response of a parent. It's important to remember that we can't always predict what our children will do or say. We can, however, learn to manage our emotional responses to that behavior.

For some parents, mental health conditions may be a key factor in their expression of anger. Intermittent explosive disorder, borderline personality disorder, and conduct disorder are all examples of anger problems that have roots in mental health. Managing these disorders can require support from medical professionals.

DIFFERENT KINDS OF ANGER

Think you know when you're acting out in anger? Think again. Anger manifests in many ways, and you may not even be aware of what's going on inside you. There are several types of anger, including:

Explosive anger

This type of anger is the most obvious. As the term suggests, this anger is characterized by volatility. You don't even know what you might say or do. One can imagine that children of parents with explosive anger will often feel fearful of these major displays of emotion. An explosively angry person may deny they have a problem.

Pain-based anger

Has your child ever told you they hate you? Or that you're the worst parent in the world? Those words hurt, even when they come from a tiny kid. When we feel emotional pain, we may experience anger. Some people find this type of anger easier to show than vulnerability.

Passive-aggressive anger

Maybe you're thinking, *Wait a minute. I never raise my voice. I never throw things. I never once called my child a little monster (at least not out loud!).* But passive-aggressive anger can be just as damaging to a child-parent bond as it signals you've been repressing your anger for quite some time. If you find yourself being sarcastic with your kid, you're likely experiencing passive-aggressive anger.

Fear-based anger

If your kid has ever run across the street just as a car is passing by, you may have shouted something like, "What's wrong with you? Why would you not look before you cross?" In this situation, you've expressed fear-based anger. Deep inside, you were terrified that your child almost got run over. Instead of acknowledging that fear, you let anger take charge.

DEALING WITH ANGER

Who knew there was so much anger out there in the world? But alas, it's there. And when some of that anger comes from you, it's up to you to do something about it.

Note that managing your anger doesn't mean bottling it up. When your child is punching your arm because you won't let them watch a third hour of the world's loudest kids show, no one expects you to just smile.

However, there are some tricks that can make dealing with your anger easier.

Laugh about it! Sometimes, we have to laugh at our child's actions or even our own reactions. We've all seen that viral video of the two kids busting into their father's formal BBC interview. If *those* parents can find the humor, so can you.

Work out your anger. Melt away that anger with a HIIT workout or a P90X subscription.

Don't take your kid's negative behavior personally. It's easy to think your child is trying to push your buttons. They're really not.

Share your parenting experience. Support groups for parent survivors of the 2022 Broccoli Tantrum or the 2020 Broken Vase incident can make a world of difference. You're not alone!

Practice breathwork. Deep breathing that starts in the diaphragm can relax your body and help you find peace, even amid chaos.

Find solutions for the root problem. Is your kid refusing to sleep because they're drinking soda with dinner? Do they not want to go to school because someone's teasing them? Identifying the root of the problem can prevent potential triggers from occurring.

UNDERSTANDING HOW ANGER AFFECTS YOUR HEALTH

Coming to terms with your anger is important for both your physical and mental health. If you allow anger to constantly bubble up inside you, it will begin to show in toxic ways.

Think back to a time when you were especially angry. Do you remember how you felt? Did you feel that icy-cold fight-or-flight instinct? That's likely because your body started pumping out stress hormones.

Each time you get angry, your heart responds by pumping faster. Your blood pressure also increases. As you might imagine, long-term exposure to these conditions isn't good for your heart in the long run. You become more at risk for serious complications like a heart attack or stroke.

There's another big downside. Your immune system starts to go haywire. It's not as effective, which means you get sick more often. And let's be real. Your kid's probably bringing home a million bugs and viruses from school, daycare, and extracurricular activities. When your immune system is malfunctioning, you're going to catch those germs more easily.

You might also find you're getting more stomach aches. Have you ever gotten so upset that you've felt sick to your stomach? All those minute processes your body undergoes in the midst of anger can create chaos in your digestive system.

The next time you have an angry episode, take note of your stomach and chest. You might be tightening your abdominal or neck muscles. There's a good chance you're breathing irregularly, too. Maybe your skin is flushed and sweaty. Perhaps you feel clammy. These are all physical signs that what you're feeling inside is stressing your body out.

What about the mental problems that recurrent anger can cause or make worse? Those can be especially hard to deal with. Conditions like anxiety and depression are much more difficult to move past than the common cold. If you're a person living with generalized anxiety disorder, anger can make your anxiety levels skyrocket. You may end up worrying about your children's health and behavior to an excessive degree.

It's probably no shock that if you're overly anxious and depressed, you might lash out or get snippy with loved ones. While everyone slips up now and then, regularly being out of control is toxic to your body and your relationships.

HOW ANGER AFFECTS RELATIONSHIPS

If you think letting your anger boil over is a healthy way of "getting it all out," that's a mistake. Think of your child's face when you yell at them. They likely appear hurt, sad, and probably scared. When your child begins to feel that way regularly when interacting with you, it's only natural that they're going to want to pull away from you. That can happen now or years into the future.

Consider Lacey's story. Lacey grew up with a mother, Diane, who often criticized her every move. Her mom had unrealistic expectations of her and was very passive-aggressive throughout her childhood. When Lacey became a parent herself, she found that she was on edge around her own mom, especially when it was the three of them all together.

Lacey noticed that when Diane was around, she became especially concerned that her daughter was going to do something that the grandmother would critique. She didn't want Diane to treat her daughter the way Lacey had been treated.

As a result, Lacey started criticizing her daughter's actions and would become disproportionately angry over her daughter's every "mistake." She became angry that her daughter took too long to tie her shoes. She was upset that she made a "C" on her book report despite spending all week working on it.

Even though Lacey's actions initially came from a good place, the resulting consequences were the same. Her daughter eventually became tense around her, and the anger cycle continued throughout the generations.

But your child's not the only one affected by these explosions. Your partner can also feel the strain, too. They may worry that you're going to hurt them or your child. They may get sick of hearing you shout all the time. What kills romance in a heartbeat? Getting constantly berated for everyday slip-ups. Or watching your partner morph into a big, angry monster in the blink of an eye.

In the worst-case scenario, you may become so out of control that your actions result in physical or emotional abuse. Obviously, this is a no-go zone. Anger is never an excuse to harm someone, and it's your responsibility to control it.

Maybe you're thinking, *I don't let my emotions erupt all over the place. I'm actually GREAT at keeping them inside so no one knows how I'm feeling.* While your first instinct might be to commend yourself on your ability to remain stoic in an ire-inducing situation, remember that managing your emotions appropriately isn't the same as swallowing them and pretending they don't exist.

Repressing your anger can be just as unhealthy as anger explosions. If you keep your anger inside you but take no action to deal with it, that anger won't magically disappear. It will stay with you like a nasty bout of indigestion until you decide what to do with it.

Repressed anger often comes out in the form of passive aggression. That might mean you intentionally don't pay a bill to get back at your partner. Or you might say things like, "I guess your friend Sophie's going to Disneyland because she's been a good little girl. Doesn't look like you'll be going any time soon."

THINGS TO WATCH OUT FOR

I know you may be feeling uncomfortable taking such a close look at yourself. No one enjoys admitting they've made mistakes. But remember, the point here isn't to make you feel racked with guilt. You've picked up this book so you can stop doing certain behaviors or prevent yourself from reaching a point of no return.

No matter what, it's necessary to take a moment to check in with yourself and reflect on your actions. This way, you can gauge where you currently stand in terms of anger management. Some signs that you may not be managing your anger the right way include:

- Blowing up over even minor mishaps or conflict
- Experiencing some of the physical/mental effects listed above
- Impulsively doing things you wouldn't do if you were content
- Expecting perfection from others and, subsequently, criticizing too much
- Exhibiting explosive rage (such as breaking or throwing things)

If any of these points sound like you, your red flag should be going up. That flag says, "Hey, I need to work on something here." It can also signal that you need more anger management tools to add to your mental toolbox.

Never fear. We've got more tools below and in the remaining chapters than a home improvement store!

WHAT HEALTHY ANGER EXPRESSION LOOKS LIKE

Okay, so you've got a pretty clear idea of what you shouldn't be doing when you're angry (i.e., Don't throw the salad bowl against the cabinet because your kid is picking out their carrots. Don't call your kid a mistake or tell them they ruined your chance to become a runway model. Don't blow up when they lose a library book. You get the idea.)

So what are some things that we <u>should</u> do when we feel angry?

We can go for a run and push ourselves like we're training for a marathon. Play a fast-paced game of racquetball with a friend and sweat out that annoyance. Join a local basketball or soccer team. Whatever it takes to work out that adrenaline and get to the point where you feel calm again.

You can also schedule a chat session with a friend. Go meet your BFF for coffee and swap horror stories from the day. If you're limited on time, a virtual chat session can work just as well. You can tell your friend, "Hey, I'm in crisis mode. I need a couple of minutes of adult time so I don't lose my sh*t." Any true best friend will answer that call ASAP.

Are you the perpetual problem solver? Jump into action when you get upset. Develop a detailed plan of action for handling your toddler's meltdown. Share the plan with your partner and encourage them to remind you of your plan. Don't forget that a kind, supportive partner is one of the best resources out there! They've likely seen the extent of your rage and are eager to help you return to your tranquil self.

You can even get your kids involved in your anger management. Of course, you don't have to go into all the grown-up stuff about why you're working on managing your emotions. You can simply say something like, "I want to hear what sorts of things work better for you." Take a tip from actress Blake Lively and leave a comment box around your house. Your kids can write a message letting you know something they liked that you did or something they didn't like. It's a low-key way to start acknowledging what is and isn't working in the household!

Remember, too, that we're in the acknowledgment phase of our anger management "training." One of the most productive things you can do when you're feeling incredibly irritated is to acknowledge that you're upset. Leave behind all the guilt, shame, and annoyance. Whatever it is you feel about your anger, let it go. Accept that you're downright MAD that your child just kicked your brand-new television, and let it be. Seriously, it's okay.

Now that you're familiar with the many ways anger can manifest, we'll take a look at some positive parenting techniques that can help eliminate triggers in Chapter 2.

Chapter Takeaways:

- Different people can exhibit various reactions to the same situations. Some people may react with anger, while others may not.
- There are many kinds of anger. Identifying which types of anger you experience will help you understand your triggers.
- Certain ways of managing your anger are healthier than others. Repressing your anger or blowing up are unhealthy ways of dealing with your feelings.

2

DISCIPLINE WITH A SMILE

> "So often children are punished for being human. Children are not allowed to have grumpy moods, bad days, disrespectful tones, or bad attitudes. Yet, us adults have them all the time. None of us are perfect. We must stop holding our children to a higher standard of perfection than we can attain ourselves."
>
> — REBECCA EANES

THE IMPORTANCE OF POSITIVE REINFORCEMENT AND PRAISE

As you know by now, parenting is not as simple as requesting that your child behave appropriately and then hoping for the best. Kids are human just like us (yes, even on those days when they seem just a little more like mischievous elves trying to create pandemonium at every opportunity).

Like us, kids want to be told they're doing a good job. We all love hearing that! Imagine if you went to work every day and never got any feedback from your boss. She only acknowledges you when she has something negative to say about your work performance. If you needed to speak with her about something one day, you might consider waiting for her to critique your performance to get the chance.

Parent-child relationships are similar. You may already be familiar with the concept of a child misbehaving to get attention. Craving attention is in a child's nature. If they're only getting negative attention, they'll still take that over no attention at all.

You can probably see how this issue could snowball into your child repeating inappropriate behavior simply to say, "Hey, look at me!". Fortunately, that doesn't have to happen.

When parents practice positive reinforcement and provide plenty of praise for their children, their kids will start looking forward to those positive interactions. They'll start showing that good behavior.

Consider this scenario. Your child leaves a half-finished game on the daycare floor when you arrive to pick her up. You tell her, "I have told you a million times, don't leave messes out. Why do you keep doing that? You're being so rude to your teacher right now." She then laughs and kicks the game, turning back to see your reaction.

Haven't we all been here? Your child looks at you to see what you're going to do. It's almost like a challenge. And no one wants to be put in a situation where they're being challenged by a three-year-old.

But let's rework that scenario. Imagine you walk into the daycare and notice your child put up a teddy bear before starting that game. If you say something like, "Wow! You put away that toy just like we've talked about. That is awesome!" they'll probably start beaming and then trying to clean up everything in sight.

Does positive reinforcement sound like bribing your kid? It's a little different than offering them a bribe because they don't know for certain how you're going to respond afterward. They show the behavior that you want and simply feel good when you praise them.

There are tons of parenting styles out there, and many of them emphasize using positive reinforcement.

A parenting style is the system (or "climate") you raise your child in. It isn't the same as a parenting practice, or a parenting action (like asking your child to do their homework before 5:00 p.m.). Parenting styles are based on demandingness (how a parent ensures their child behaves the way they expect) and responsiveness (how aware a parent is of their kid's needs).

Some examples of parenting styles include:

- **Authoritative parenting**: High demandingness, high responsiveness
- **Authoritarian parenting**: High demandingness, low responsiveness

- **Permissive parenting**: Low demandingness, high responsiveness
- **Neglectful parenting**: Low demandingness, low responsiveness

Keep in mind that children have different temperaments. This means that parents may choose to use a particular parenting approach to match that temperament. However, evidence suggests that the authoritative parenting approach is typically best for most children.

What's the authoritative parenting approach?

Don't worry. It's not actually as heartless as it sounds. It simply means that parents expect a lot of their children but are also compassionate toward them. For example, you may tell your child you expect them to feed the dog by 7:00 a.m. each day, but you also explain your reasoning. You may say something like, "It's important you feed the dog because everyone in our family contributes to household chores. And when you feed the dog by 7:00, you won't need to rush to get to school on time."

The authoritative parenting approach makes use of positive words for children. Parents who have high expectations of their children but who also demonstrate high responsiveness may say things like:

- "I'm very proud of you."
- "Let's give your way a try."
- "I love spending time together."
- "You need a break like everyone else does."

And don't be afraid to joke with your child! Yes, it's possible to be an authoritative parent while still maintaining a sense of humor. In fact, smiling and laughing with your kid is a fantastic way to bond. So go ahead and share your best mom or dad jokes with them. (Need one? Here you go: "What sounds like a sneeze and is made of leather? A shoe." You're welcome!)

You can even share funny stories from when you were young. The point is to bond with your kid and take advantage of those fun, carefree moments.

STRATEGIES FOR EFFECTIVE DISCIPLINE WITHOUT ANGER

Authoritative parenting is very similar to a concept known as gentle parenting. Gentle parenting, as the name suggests, emphasizes raising your children in a loving, caring environment. You show your kid directly that you care about them and respond with kindness instead of anger.

Here's an example. Imagine your child accidentally drops their plate of food as they're leaving the dinner table. Instead of yelling at your kid and asking why they weren't more careful, a gentle parent might say, "Oh no, that plate didn't cut you when it broke, did it? I've broken a few dishes myself. I'll help you clean up the mess."

Not too hard, right?

Gentle parenting is not only a simple idea but one that has tons of benefits. Kids who tend to be on the shyer end may be able to interact with others a little easier. We all know kids soak up their environment, for better or worse. Just ask any parent who has ever accidentally let out a swear word and heard their toddler casually repeat it in public.

Fortunately, the same goes for those positive traits we want to pass on to our kids. When we parent gently, we teach kids to treat others with compassion. They'll absorb those kind habits and spread them to others.

Don't confuse gentle parenting with permissive parenting. A parent who uses the gentle approach still lays out clear boundaries for their child. There is no doubt about expectations. If discipline becomes necessary, the course of action comes from a loving but firm place. For parents who have trouble controlling their anger, gentle parenting will take practice.

Let's take a look at some discipline strategies that an authoritative, or gentle, parent might use.

Keep in mind that discipline methods should vary according to your child's age. Take a look at your current discipline methods and see if they're age appropriate. An infant or a one-year-old who keeps pulling your hair isn't going to understand time out. But you can certainly distract them with a toy or a new setting. However, the distraction strategy isn't going to work on a five-year-old who tears up their sister's book on purpose. In this case, a five-minute time-out would be appropriate.

For younger children, it's especially important to show them that you mean business when it comes to discipline. No, this doesn't mean you must make them scared of you. It *does* mean that they need to know you intend to follow through on the consequences of their unacceptable behaviors.

For elementary or middle-school-aged children, you can give them a warning if they've done something they shouldn't do. At this point, you can give them a very clear idea of what will happen if the behavior is repeated. For example, you can say, "If you throw that toy across the room one more time, I will put it away so you can't play with it anymore." When the child throws it again, follow through. Calmly put the toy away as you said you would.

It can be helpful to explain why you're disciplining the child in this way. The moment you take that toy from them, you will likely hear something along the lines of "You're so mean!" or "Why did you do that?" This is the perfect chance to tell them, "I wasn't being mean. I was doing what I told you would happen if you threw the toy again. Someone might get hurt when you're throwing things."

Teenagers are a whole different consideration. Disciplining teenagers is more like guiding them. By the time a child is fifteen or sixteen, they have a better understanding of your expectations and can even be involved in the rule-making process. We all know how turbulent the teenage years can be thanks to our own personal experience. Be sure to call attention to the great things your teen does. While they likely want to be an adult, they're still kids at heart. They want to know their parents are proud of them and that they have made a positive impact at school and in the family.

When it comes to teenagers, finding a good balance between overprotectiveness and the free-range approach can help them exhibit healthy behaviors. Many of your current instances of anger may stem from a desire to protect your teen from the bad parts of life. While you'll of course want to protect them, as they grow closer to adulthood, you'll need to help them find ways to manage situations on their own.

Listen to them and learn why they might have trouble meeting your expectations. This is a good way to help them learn to problem-solve. For instance, why is your son failing Algebra? Is he having a hard time hearing because the two students beside him keep talking throughout the lesson? Is he struggling to finish his math homework because he's busy with the track team and band practice?

A clear line of communication can help prevent further problems down the road while teaching your child how to navigate life's tricky situations. While it can seem like your child's toddler years were an eternity ago, remember that they're really not so different these days. Children want to know their parents love them, even when they make mistakes. As children grow, the consequences of those mistakes grow bigger, so it's essential to adopt a gentle parenting method to lead them in the right direction.

MANAGING ANGER IN CHALLENGING SITUATIONS

With all these strategies under your belt, you're probably feeling ready to conquer the parenting world. But you still need to make that jump from experiencing a trigger (like your child not following the rules) to gently disciplining *without* dissolving into anger.

Easier said than done, I know. With practice, you'll get there, though!

A key component of managing your anger is figuring out why your kid is "acting out." Most of the time, there is a logical explanation. Think about it this way. You have had decades of experience figuring out how to express yourself, while your child is still new to the game. Sometimes, a child may be throwing a tantrum because they have a pebble in their shoe and are too young to realize it. They may also be too young to fix the problem (i.e., they can't untie and retie their shoes yet). You'd be pretty unhappy walking around like that all day, too!

Another common reason kids start to have meltdowns is when they're not feeling well. It's tempting to get mad when your daughter or son starts to flip out for seemingly no reason. But it could be that they have a fever, stomachache, or another illness. Young children often don't know how to put their physical ailments into words, and you'll need to be on the lookout for signs like tantrums and picking fights with their siblings. Yelling is a form of communication after all; although, not the preferred one for parents with good hearing!

Similarly, kids with ADHD, social anxiety, or other conditions may be triggered by certain situations. For instance, a child who is socially anxious may do everything in their power to delay going to school or a party. Take note of these types of patterns and follow up with a medical professional if you suspect your child may need an assessment.

Your child may also keep acting out because they learned it works. You may not want to admit it but consider whether you give into your kid's "bad" behavior simply to stop the tantrum. There's no shame in not wanting to hear your child scream and being tempted to give them the second scoop of ice cream they're demanding (especially when they're demanding loudly . . . in public). However, not standing firm will reinforce the idea that tantrums are a fantastic tool for getting what they want!

Public tantrums are especially difficult for many parents. Not only are all eyes on you because your kid is wailing about wanting every item on the shelf, but you may feel particularly pressured to get your kid to stop as quickly as possible.

The biggest trick to avoiding getting angry is to prevent the issue from escalating. Here are some ideas to do just that:

- Eliminate the problem. When the cause of the problem is obvious, don't be afraid to choose the easiest solution. For example, if your son won't put on his jacket because he says it's too itchy, let him wear a different jacket. Or cut out the tag if that's bothering him. Or help him choose his comfiest sweater to put on under his jacket. Don't get stuck on the idea that he must absolutely wear the exact thing you picked out.
- Communicate. In the heat of the moment, it can be easy to forget to communicate with your child. Don't forget to *ask* them what they need. Take a moment to ask them what might help them feel better. You may be surprised at what your child is upset about ("I'm crying at the bank because I miss Daddy.")
- Set clear expectations. Many of us grew up hearing phrases like "Be a good girl!" or "Be on your best behavior." These sorts of statements are too

subjective to be useful. Tell your child clearly what you expect. "Sadie, share the soccer ball with your friends on the playground." or "Finish your assignments in class."

- Use positive reinforcement. When your child does something you appreciate, let them know. They'll be more inclined to do it next time. You could say, "I really appreciate how you helped your brother get ready to go out for dinner. That helped him, and it helped me, too!"
- Reward good behavior. One fast way to get your kids to stick to your expectations is by offering a reward. Let them have a say in what exactly the reward is, whether it's going to their favorite ice cream shop or watching a movie at home. This way, you can be sure the reward is appealing to them.

SETTING AND MAINTAINING BOUNDARIES IN A POSITIVE WAY

Another important component of gentle and authoritative parenting is to set healthy boundaries for your children. Setting a boundary means establishing a clear distinction between you as a parent and your son or daughter as the child. While you should certainly have a good time with your child, they should never consider your relationship simply a friendship.

Setting boundaries can help you keep your sanity and ensure your kid is getting to live their own life. Some parents may worry so much about whether their child is going to succeed in school, they may do projects for them or complete homework assignments for them. This is an example of something called over-functioning.

Over-functioning parents are also those parents who push their kids into all those activities they never got the chance to do. Obviously, you want what's best for your child. But if you end up living through them instead of letting them live as their own person, this will cause problems in your relationship. (Do you remember Amy Poehler's character in *Mean Girls*? The "cool" mom? She's the definition of a parent who has let boundaries fly out the window.)

Your child needs your guidance but they also need some autonomy to make their own choices and to learn from their mistakes.

How do you go about setting boundaries? If you're realizing that you and your children have been crossing each other's boundaries, you might not know where to begin. It's never too late, though!

You can start now. Specifically state what is and isn't all right. Try phrases like "It's not okay to hit me. Ever." or "It's okay to tell me when you're worried about something." Remember, these boundaries are to help both you and your kid.

You can request that they knock before entering your room. Tell your child that when you say "No" to something, you mean it, and it's not up for negotiation. Another example of setting boundaries is telling them name-calling is not allowed in your household. Explain that you won't be calling them names, and they won't be calling you names.

When everyone respects these boundaries, your family will begin to feel less volatile and more peaceful. Don't we all want that?

CHECKLIST TO HELP YOU STOP YELLING AT YOUR KIDS

Here are some of the top things you can do when you feel like you're losing your mind around your kids.

- Apologize for yelling at them. Virtually every parent has yelled at some point, and letting your child know you make mistakes too can create a healthier relationship.
- Avoid triggers as much as possible. Have your partner read the bedtime books if you get annoyed when your kid makes up every last excuse to not sleep. If your child drives you crazy as you're preparing their lunch, let them prepare their own lunch, and then you can adjust it later as needed.
- Form different expectations. Is it possible that you might be expecting too much of your child? Familiarize yourself with what's normal behavior for your child's age. This can help you have fewer meltdowns.

Now that you know what gentle and authoritative parenting entails, let's dive into ways we can navigate those unavoidable triggers.

Chapter Takeaways:

- Children respond well to positive reinforcement and praise.
- Authoritative parenting is an evidence-based approach that emphasizes establishing boundaries while being emotionally responsive.
- Managing anger can be difficult, especially in public settings. There are many strategies you can use to avoid becoming overwhelmed in these situations.

3

NAVIGATING PARENTING TRIGGERS

"Instead of treating your child like how you were treated, treat them with the same love and attention you wanted from your parents while growing up."

— JONATHAN ANTHONY BURKETT, NEGLECTED BUT UNDEFEATED: THE LIFE OF A BOY WHO NEVER KNEW A MOTHER'S LOVE

Recognizing that there are certain things that trigger you is essential. This way, you can be on the lookout for those troublesome situations. For instance, maybe you dread bath time because every time it rolls around, your daughter starts kicking and screaming, refusing to wash herself. In response, you start yelling and threatening to take away every privilege under the sun or throw away all her toys. Not a fun scene to replay night after night, is it?

Didn't think so.

The more you learn about your triggers and your responses to them, the easier it becomes to react the way you want to them. Imagine that. Reacting how you want to, even in a stressful situation. Consider that same bath scenario, but this time, instead of yelling when your child refuses to bathe, you calmly tell them, "It's important that you bathe at 8:00 p.m. so that we can have plenty of time for bedtime stories. We might even have time for *two* stories if you get in the tub right away."

WHAT NOT TO DO WHEN ANGER STRIKES

Certain things won't help the situation when those triggering moments overwhelm you. There are four major things you want to avoid doing:

- **Don't yell.** Yelling is a lot more exhausting than speaking in a calm, serious tone. Your child will also be more likely to understand what you're saying when you're explaining yourself peacefully.
- **Don't use physical aggression.** Never resort to hitting your child. It's not effective, and it can damage your relationship with them.
- **Don't use hurtful language.** When you call your kid names, you're not only showing your immaturity, but you're hurting their self-esteem.
- **Don't discipline in the heat of the moment.** It can be tempting to shout and tell them they're grounded for a year. Obviously, that's not a great strategy.

Waiting until you've cooled down lets you consider appropriate consequences.

When you resort to these tactics, you invite even more problems into your home. Your child may react immediately to these tactics and stop their negative behavior, but you're setting up a long-term problem. Children can become emotionally traumatized by constant yelling. And if you go on a very long tirade, your kid is going to start tuning you out.

It stands to reason your kid will be more reluctant to tell you about problems they're having because they're worried you will start yelling or blame them. This can lead to long-term problems in your relationship, with your child ultimately withdrawing from you completely.

Even worse, your child may go on to continue this cycle of anger with their own children. Wouldn't you rather nip the anger in the bud?

I know you're probably sitting there thinking, okay, if I can't yell, spank, or tell my kid they're being a little punk, what *can* I do? Fortunately, there are a lot of effective strategies that can help you keep your calm. By managing your anger, you can think through your reaction rather than just exploding.

If you're confronted with a stressful situation, such as your daughter screaming at you, you can walk away. Yes, it's completely okay. If she is not doing anything dangerous, you can walk away and take a moment to yourself. Use the opportunity to count to ten. Ten seconds gives you a long enough pause to collect your thoughts and think before you say something you might regret.

You can also try deep breathing exercises or talking with a friend. Our friends have a way of helping us see the humorous side of our children's behavior. Somehow, having to say out loud, "My daughter called me a big butthead this morning, and I got so mad I told her she couldn't watch *Daniel Tiger* for two days," can even help dissolve your anger.

You can even develop a playlist for those tense moments. Compile your favorite happy, upbeat songs that never fail to get you in a good mood.

THE DOWNFALLS OF "OLD-SCHOOL" PUNISHMENT

Unfortunately, there are certain methods that have been traditionally used by parents, including yelling and physical discipline, that are still used today. As we've discussed, science shows that these strategies simply aren't effective.

Some parents argue that their parents spanked them or yelled at them "and they turned out just fine." Chances are, you've been affected by these discipline methods more than you think. Researchers have found that punishing children can create resentment in children to the extent that they'll distance themselves from you.

Kids who are spanked are more at risk for showing aggression at school, while kids whose parents repeatedly yell at them are likelier to lie and steal. These children learn to think more about themselves than others. For example, your son may realize he will get a spanking if you learn he stole candy from the store, but that doesn't help instill the idea that stealing is wrong. Instead, it only encourages him to lie about it to avoid getting hit. A better approach would be to explain how theft affects the store's business and how his actions hurt someone in the long run.

Let's examine another example you may encounter. What if you want your child to get ready for a holiday get-together at your brother's house? Your kid keeps dragging her feet and putting off getting dressed. If you're using a dangerous "old-school" parenting style, you may spank her and tell her she needs to get her act together. She may go and get dressed, but you can bet that she's going to be sobbing and show up to the party in a not-so-great mood. The party your whole family has been looking forward to for weeks is now ruined because your kid can't enjoy it, and you feel guilty for spanking her.

A healthier alternative for you both would have been to calmly explain to your daughter why getting dressed on time is important. You could have said something like, "Your uncle has asked us to come at 6:00 p.m. because he cooked us a special meal. We want to show him how thankful we are that he took the time to cook your favorite mac and cheese. He will be so disappointed if he puts all that special work into cooking for you and you don't get to eat it."

Esther Wojcicki is an educator and journalist who wrote *How to Raise Successful People*, a bestselling book that emphasizes treating your children with kindness and avoiding helicopter parenting. She stresses that effective parenting focuses on teaching your child the importance of community. Kids who volunteer are less likely to break the law. Doesn't showing your child how to mow your neighbor's lawn, for example, sound much more appealing than screaming your head off at them for hours? I think so!

You can also model the type of language you want your kid to use rather than resorting to an outdated punishment method. When your kid accidentally steps on your foot, are you the type of parent who yells, "Watch what you're doing? Don't act stupid!"? If so, you can plan on getting talked to that same way by your child. Who can blame them? They're learning the English language from you, after all.

While it's a natural reaction to yell "Ow!" when you're hurt, you can control yourself and say, "Please don't run around me. That really hurt when you stepped on me. This is why I asked you not to run inside." This calm approach teaches your kid that you respect them, and in turn, they will respect you.

PRACTICAL TECHNIQUES FOR DISARMING YOUR TRIGGERS

As the example we just discussed shows, for many people, pain is a prime trigger for anger. We're tempted to use our anger to show, "Hey! That hurt! Don't do that again!" In today's modern world, we don't have to turn to aggression to explain our feelings. Instead, we can use plain old language that helps get our ideas across. That's right—no need to go caveman and yell when our kid hurts us. We've got the ability to speak in more than one syllable at a time!

What are some other common triggers besides pain?

- **Work stress:** No one feels their best after a long, hard day at the office. If you come home to a house your teenager has virtually destroyed, you may be very triggered.
- **Medical issues**: If you are living with a chronic illness or have simply been feeling under the weather, you may find yourself getting angrier more than usual.
- **Traffic:** Who hasn't felt incredibly frustrated as they've sat in a major traffic jam on the freeway? That's why we hear so many horns blaring for no reason while sitting at a standstill.
- **Embarrassment:** You won't catch many parents smiling when their kid says, "Hey Dad, why do you look so fat today?" in the middle of a school meeting. Many people will lash out in anger at this type of comment.
- **Sadness:** Having trouble expressing emotions like sadness and grief is not unusual. Sometimes, it's easier to let out your anger rather than tell people how you're really feeling: incredibly depressed.
- **Exhaustion:** Have you ever snapped when you were just really tired? It's more common than you think.

Once you realize you're in one of those volatile moments and your anger starts rearing its ugly head, you can do a couple of things. First, you can stop yourself at that initial crossroads. You know the one I'm talking about. The one where one sign points to a place called "All Hell Breaks Loose & There's No Turning Back" and another sign that points to "The Peaceful Route a Therapist Would Recommend."

Take a moment to breathe and **acknowledge** that you're feeling triggered. Remember that you've been to "All Hell Breaks Loose & There's No Turning Back" many, many times, and like that one town in Idaho where your in-laws live, you're never going back. Instead, venture down that peaceful route. The one where you're reminded, "Oh, yeah. It's not a big deal if my daughter doesn't eat all her spaghetti tonight. She might just not be hungry."

You can also try to be logical about the situation. Just like those people beeping their horns in gridlocked traffic, showing your anger in drastic ways makes zero sense. It only makes you expend more energy and, honestly, makes you look pretty foolish. If you're upset that your son left his backpack at the foot of the stairs again, do you *really* need to stomp up to his room like a big, grouchy monster? Or can you just calmly ask him to please pick it up so no one trips on it?

Listen to your anger. No, I don't mean listen to that fire-breathing dragon voice that comes out of your mouth when someone doesn't clean the hair out of the shower drain. I mean, listen to what your anger is saying *inside of you*. When you walk through the door after an infuriating meeting with your boss, are you carrying that little flame of fire with you? Are you really wanting to shout at your boss for thinking you can do 60 hours of work in 40? If you're spreading this anger to others, you'll need to address that little flame at work rather than letting it become a wildfire at home.

COPING STRATEGIES WHEN ANGER IS UNAVOIDABLE

Big changes take time. If you've been living the angry life for years, you've learned many negative habits that will take a while to unlearn. You may find there are moments when you simply can't help being mad. You feel that rage start to boil up within you.

That's okay if you're not able to prevent anger.

This book isn't about learning to be a saintly parent or a robotic one that has Stepford wife vibes. Instead, I want to help you learn to deal with that inevitable anger that makes us all human. You can't necessarily help your automatic reactions to a situation, but you can 100% choose how you deal with existing anger.

We've talked about using deep breathing exercises to control our emotions. Let's take a deeper look at some specific techniques we can use when that wave of anger overcomes us, whether it's in the carpool line at school or at soccer practice when your child has a meltdown because her team lost.

If you're familiar with yoga, you may know the term pranayama (pronounced: prah-nah-YAH-mah), or breathing practice. This Sanskrit term refers to using your breath as a means to gain control of yourself. There are several pranayama types, including:

Nadi shodhana breathing (pronounced: nah-DEE show-DAH-nah): This is alternate nostril breathing. You can put one thumb over one nostril and breathe in through the free nostril. Before letting the breath out, place a thumb over the other nostril, and let the air out. You can feel reenergized and more awake.

Adham pranayama (pronounced: ahd-HAHM prah-nah-YAH-mah): Also called belly breathing, this type is characterized by placing one hand on your belly while you're sitting straight up. Feel your belly expand and contract as you breathe. Adham pranayama can help alleviate anxiety.

Kapalabhati breathing (pronounced: kah-pah-lah-BAH-tee): This pranayama is known as "skull-shining breath." To do it, simply take a long breath in and then force the air out through a quick exhale. The exhale should start in your lower belly. Like nadi shodhana breathing, this technique can help you feel energized.

Another useful strategy for relaxing in the moment is using guided visualization. When you feel especially upset, take a moment to yourself and listen to a specially designed recording. Therapists often use this technique with patients, which can help people find their "happy place" even when they're feeling angry.

You can step into a bathroom and splash cold water on your face. Your face is likely beginning to warm as you get angry, and cooling it down with water can help your body remember what it's like to feel calm again. This technique can also help you take that extra ten seconds to calm down.

You can even take a few moments to journal out your frustration. You don't have to whip out an actual diary. Even a sticky note or scrap of paper will work. Scribble out your frustrations and either keep your note to reflect on later or tear it up and throw it away. Tearing up those negative emotions can feel pretty darn good!

ARE YOU AN EFFECTIVE PARENT?

There are days when you're probably wondering if you're doing any good for your child. The term "effective parent" is used to describe parents who not only meet their children's basic needs but also make a constant effort to connect with their children. Effective parents also help their kids grow up to be great people.

The Center for Parenting Education has a practical list of questions you can use to help you determine whether you are currently an effective parent. Some of the questions you can use to gauge your effectiveness are:

- ☐ Do my kids know ahead of time what will happen if they misbehave?
- ☐ Am I helping my children become outstanding adults?
- ☐ Do I take time out of my day (every day) to bond with my kid?
- ☐ Do the consequences I give my children fit the situation?
- ☐ Am I setting a good example for my children?
- ☐ Do I discuss their behavior when I'm calm?

The more questions you can check off and answer "yes" to, the more likely it is that you are an effective parent. Refer to this list every now and then to hold yourself accountable and remind yourself to go the extra mile with your child.

Learning to acknowledge when your anger is looming is a skill that takes time. Practice the strategies we've discussed in this chapter and start implementing them today. When you feel comfortable acknowledging your anger, turn to the next chapter. Here, we'll discuss tips for disengaging from a tough situation.

Chapter Takeaways:

- Never spank or yell at your kids. They're short-term solutions that can cause long-term harm.
- Know your triggers and identify what you're really mad at.
- Breathing exercises are simple to do and can calm you down quickly.

STEP 2: DISENGAGE AND DEFUSE THE SITUATION

4

THE POWER OF STEPPING AWAY

"Anger is like a storm rising up from the bottom of your consciousness. When you feel it coming, turn your focus to your breath."

— THICH NHAT HANH

In the first three chapters, you've learned a lot about the different types of anger. You've also learned how to recognize and avoid your triggers when possible. In Chapter 4, I'll discuss some in-depth strategies for stepping away from those situations that make you irate. I'll also talk about ways you can regulate your emotions and recenter yourself, even when you're feeling like you're out of control.

Keep in mind that one of the best ways (if not *the* best way) to help your child become a person in control of their actions is to model that behavior. Your child looks up to you and wants to be like you in more ways than you'll ever know. Even if you're guilty of doing some not-so-great things as a parent, they still want to please you and follow in your footsteps more often than not.

When the going gets tough, remember that you're working on your anger management skills not just for yourself but for your child, too. And if you want to get really meta about it, think of it as helping your grandchildren, and your great-grandchildren, and so on. You are creating a positive family environment for generations down the road because these parenting traits get passed down through the centuries.

Now that you've got the pressure of your whole family line weighing on you (kidding!), let's dive in!

STEPPING AWAY FROM ANGER

A big obstacle to dealing with anger is being able to get enough distance from your emotions in the heat of the moment. After all, anger is one of the few emotions that can get people's immediate attention. In fact, anger can even be good sometimes, when handled appropriately. If we get angry at ourselves for making a mistake, it encourages us to do better next time. If we calmly express our displeasure at something our partner said, they'll take care to speak more politely next time.

But triggered anger, which is the kind parents usually deal with, needs to be handled a lot differently. Our feelings may be hurt or we may feel frustrated, and acting in the moment can create devastating effects on the relationship you have with your child.

Learning to step away from your anger is a way to keep your anger in check. In other words, it helps you control your anger instead of the other way around. Your children will feel more comfortable knowing you are in control of your emotions. Put yourself in their shoes for a moment and imagine what they see when you're in a rage. You're probably moving around wildly and practically steaming at the ears. They're not likely to be worried about becoming a better person at that moment. Instead, they're probably watching your every move to see what you're going to do, just like you might do if you encountered a rabid dog.

No one wants to be the rabid, unpredictable parent!

To help your kids know what to expect of you, you'll first need to figure that out yourself. What are you going to do when you're so mad you could scream? Are you going to:

- **Take a timeout?** Believe it or not, adults can benefit from timeouts, too! Just like you separate a temperamental kindergartener from others on the playground, you should separate yourself from your kids and your partner. Set a timer on your phone for five minutes or even longer. You can say something like, "I'm going to take a five-minute break to calm down. Then I'll be back, and we can talk about this."
- **Remove yourself from the situation?** Sometimes, you need a little more space than a brief timeout allows. You can go for a walk around the house or the block and get some fresh air. A change of scenery can be great for the mind. It'll be much harder to feel angry when your neighbor waves at you from across the road.

- **Find the humor?** Take a second to laugh about the situation if you can. You may not immediately feel like there is anything remotely funny about it, but if you actively seek out something funny, I guarantee you'll find it. Maybe it's the way your daughter painted on her eyebrows when she broke into your makeup drawer. Perhaps you find it funny that your son thought sneaking out of the house was a smart idea when you have an alarm system set.

A relaxing game plan that works for one person may not work for you. For instance, the chatty mom at the park may love to get together with her besties once a week to vent about their children and swap stories. But when the weekend rolls around, you may prefer to hire a babysitter and have a date night with your spouse to intentionally talk about adult topics (no homework talk for once!).

One idea that I really like is creating a "calm down kit." This is a box filled with your favorite relaxing things. You can pull out this box whenever you need to. Have fun with stuffing it full of special items just for you. Here are some suggestions:

- Candles in calming scents (think lavender, jasmine, and peppermint)
- Puzzles with picturesque scenes (Can you really stay angry while piecing together an image of cute kittens playing with yarn?)
- Chocolates and candy (Think of this as a secret stash that neither your partner nor children know about!)
- Positive affirmations and quotes (Write down phrases that keep you going when times get tough)

- Pictures (Choose pictures that make you smile. They can be printed memes, family photos, or ones you simply think are pretty)
- Essential oil spray (Spritz a bit of essential oil in your favorite scent for a burst of tranquility)

Calm-down kits are convenient because you can make them as small or as large as you want. You can even have multiple! Stash one in your office, car, and bedroom so you can access them no matter where you are.

CHOOSING THE HIGHER GROUND: WALKING AWAY FROM A FIGHT

Many of us have been taught to never walk away from a fight. We seem to think there's a sort of honor in having the last word, being the loudest, or having the sharpest comeback. In reality, walking away from a fight takes so much more strength than giving in to your anger.

Walking away from a fight signals a strong, healthy frame of mind. You recognize that you are not your best self right now. You have acknowledged that you are triggered, and you are ready to move on to the next step in the anger management cycle: **disengaging**.

When it comes to arguing with your kids, it's especially important to walk away when you've reached your limit (ideally, well before you've reached that limit). Sometimes, kids actually like arguing because they are quite literally testing your limits. If they think there's a chance you might give in and let them stay up an extra hour or spend the night at a friend's house, they're going to try and pick a fight to achieve it.

If your kid follows you around the house to argue, you can close them out of the room. Take care of yourself at this moment, and take a breather. There's a good chance your kid will start yelling to get your attention. They might even begin to knock on the door nonstop. But in this situation, ignoring them is often the best move.

Children are intelligent creatures. They don't have much power and will wield what little they do have to their advantage. Most kids will prod you over and over to see if you cave. It can be a tough game, but they'll eventually give up.

Hold your children accountable for the things they do in fits of anger. Some kids resort to breaking objects in their room when they don't get their way. If they've damaged part of the house (like scribbling on the walls or tearing down the curtains), you can later have them pay to fix these things. The money can come from their allowance or holiday gifts.

"Walking away" in this context doesn't always mean physically leaving. It can be mentally leaving the situation for a while. For instance, if your child is trying to fight with you while driving, you may be able to distract yourself from the situation by putting on some calming music.

However, if possible, pulling over to a safe space can be a much better course of action in terms of safety. You'll want to pull over if your child is kicking the back of your seat, pulling your hair, or screaming. Tell them what you're doing and why. "I'm pulling the car over because you're behaving in a way that's making it unsafe for me to drive. When you've decided to calm down, I'll start the car again, and we can continue."

PRACTICING EMOTIONAL REGULATION & RECENTERING

Have you ever heard the term recentering? Recentering yourself means returning yourself to your normal self. When extreme emotions like anger get the best of us, we can feel out of whack. A powerful strategy for dealing with your anger is learning to regulate your emotions and recenter yourself so that you can get back to your everyday life.

Before you started reading this book, you were likely at a place in your life where you felt constantly drained by all the fighting, yelling, and daily struggles with your child. Trying to bounce back after an epic screaming match can be difficult. After all, you've expended tons of energy, and your adrenaline levels are going haywire.

Once you've learned to control your emotions, you won't feel as exhausted. However, even experiencing small amounts of controlled anger can make you feel a bit off. To get yourself in the right headspace, there are some tricks you can try.

First, you'll want to focus on minimizing your anger in the first place. Taming your emotions is called **emotional regulation**. The amount of emotional regulation you have is how well you're able to experience and express your feelings. For example, if you're someone who gets angry easily, you probably have difficulty regulating your anger. But if you're someone who never seems to get bothered by anything, you have a high level of emotional regulation.

Emotional regulation involves the things you do when you're triggered, the things you don't do when you're triggered, and how you respond when you're triggered. When you learn to control your emotions, including anger, you'll feel more confident in your ability to respond to stressful situations in appropriate and healthy ways.

Thankfully, the level of emotional regulation we have can change. That's great news, isn't it? That means that even if you have a short fuse these days, you can learn to lengthen that fuse. One day, you'll find that you don't snap when you see your child is failing a course. Instead, you'll be able to discuss the situation with them and develop an effective action plan. Doesn't strategizing about finding tutors and mentors sound like a much better solution than shouting, "I've had enough of your laziness! Go to your room!"? I have a feeling your child will respond much more positively to the first scenario.

To get a better grip on your emotions, you'll want to get a couple of skills under your belt. You'll want to learn how to:

- Create space (giving yourself a moment to calm down)
- Acknowledge what you're feeling (that includes noticing and putting a name to your emotion)
- Accept the emotion
- Stay mindful of your actions and words

Staying mindful means taking note of our surroundings and realizing what we're doing in it. What might this look like in the middle of a chaotic situation? Imagine you and your daughter are clothes shopping. You're asking your child to try on the clothes you've picked out, but she's refusing. In fact, she's getting so upset she's starting to pout and whine.

If you're mindful, you can take a moment to breathe deeply. Remember that you're simply in a clothing store. You're not in a life-or-death situation. It's not the end of the world if your child doesn't try on the pair of jeans. When you take a moment to put the scene in perspective, you'll be able to react more rationally.

Instead of snapping and saying, "You'd better try on those clothes or else!" you can recenter yourself. Adopt a peaceful frame of mind and consider why she doesn't want to try them on. Would she like to pick another outfit? Would she like to go to another store because these outfits aren't in style? Would she rather eat lunch first and come back when she's not so hungry? Even if she's just in a stubborn mood, practicing mindfulness at this moment can help you control your emotions.

Don't bother trying to control your kid's actions. It doesn't work. It never has, despite parents trying throughout history. What you can control, though, is what *you* do when they "act out."

Another way you can practice mindfulness is by creating a gratitude list. When you're feeling like a failure as a parent, take a second to write out all the things you're grateful for about your child. You might be grateful for those moments when they hug you. Maybe you're thankful you have a sweet kid who always makes sure others are okay. You could be grateful for the fact that they haven't gotten into any serious trouble in high school when so many others have.

Remembering to practice gratitude can put our relationships into perspective. It can help remind you that one bad day doesn't negate the twenty good days. No relationship is perfect, but focusing on the good can remind you how amazing the bond you have with your child is.

If you haven't tried meditation before, this technique can be another convenient way to recenter yourself. When you're feeling stressed out, find a quiet place to sit. You can sit outside in your yard, on the porch, in the house, or even lie in bed. Try to clear your mind from all thoughts (this is easier said than done, I know, but do the best you can!).

Take note of what thoughts cross your mind. When meditating, you don't want to fixate on the thoughts but instead, let them go. Spend some time in silence and note the thoughts crossing your mind. Later, after your meditation session, you can reflect on those images that kept coming to mind.

Were you worrying about your child going to summer camp? Could that worry be part of the reason you got so upset with him when he didn't call you right after school like he was supposed to? Reflecting on your meditation time can help you learn more about your inner thoughts and anxieties.

If you don't feel comfortable with complete silence, you can always try a guided meditation. There are plenty of free podcasts and YouTube videos available. Typically, these guided meditations walk you through a visualization process. Some may turn your awareness to your senses and ask you to concentrate on what you see, hear, smell, feel, and taste.

Walking meditation is also a thing! Some people have to constantly be on the move, and sitting for a long period isn't feasible. Take a quiet walk in the woods by yourself. Focus on breathing in the scent of the trees and listening to the birds singing. Feel the sunshine on your face. Notice what types of emotions you feel as you experience these simple, everyday moments.

The more you practice responding to your emotions, the easier it will get to acknowledge them and then disengage from them. Soon, you'll become more attuned to not only your emotions but your child's as well.

This leads us to the next chapter, where you will learn how to apply mindfulness to your parenting strategy. I'll explain how the mindful parenting technique can improve your relationship with your child.

Chapter Takeaways:

- Distancing yourself from your anger lets you disengage from a triggering situation.
- Walking away from a fight can help you manage your anger.
- Regulating your emotions and recentering yourself can teach you about your emotions and triggers.

5

FINDING AND UNDERSTANDING YOUR CALM

"The moment you begin to actively discover the amazing personhood of your child, parenting starts to feel like less of a burden and more of an adventure."

— ANGELA PRUESS, LICENSED CHILD THERAPIST

Let's take a deeper look at how mindfulness can make your parenting experience not only calmer but more enjoyable. While mindfulness is often associated with religions including Hinduism and Buddhism, the practice is a spiritual one that can be done by just about anyone, including parents who don't follow any religion.

You don't need to be a yoga guru or a New Age enthusiast to adopt mindful methods, and you can use the strategies that work for you and your family. Parents who use mindfulness may have an easier time keeping their emotions under control. Jon Kabat-Zinn, founder of the Stress Reduction Clinic at the University of Massachusetts Medical School, has said, "We are all mindful to one degree or another, moment by moment. It is an inherent human capacity."

IMPORTANCE OF MINDFULNESS AND BEING PRESENT

As a parent, you're under a lot of pressure. You're responsible for raising a human being. Besides providing their basic needs like food, clothing, and shelter, you're also their primary source of comfort and guidance.

It's easy to get overwhelmed and let our emotions get the best of us. When you find your anger is getting out of control, turning to mindfulness can be the key to transitioning to a peaceful, rational state. Being mindful of yourself, your actions, and your child's needs will help you recognize all the great things you're doing as a parent. It will also help you learn from your mistakes and move forward.

Because let's face it – most of us are simply too focused on being perfect parents. Perhaps you find yourself lying awake at night replaying that terrible fight you had with your teenager. Maybe you're constantly comparing yourself to other parents and wondering what you're doing wrong. While it's not a bad thing to want to improve your parenting, it won't help anyone if you're constantly beating yourself up because you're worried you've made the wrong decision or said the wrong thing.

When it comes down to it, being mindfully present in your child's life is much more important than being perfect. But what does being truly present look like?

It can mean you're attentive to your child's individuality. You recognize them as their own person rather than an extension of yourself. Being present means you're actively listening to their needs and wants *in the moment*. You aren't bringing your own judgment or preconceptions about the situation to the table. It also means you're willing to go the extra mile to keep your kid safe and happy, even when it takes a lot of work.

Instead of reacting with anger or frustration when they're throwing a tantrum, you take a moment to consider what's really happening. You might acknowledge that they're simply yelling in the middle of the living room, and that action in itself is not a big deal in the grand scheme of things. In this situation, a mindful parent takes a deep breath and considers the root cause of the child's tantrum. What do they really need? What are they trying to communicate?

Headspace, the tremendously popular mindful meditation app, states that mindful parenting "involves pausing so that you can be attuned to your child's deeper needs [. . .] and respond to them in an appropriate and loving way."

Why is mindful parenting so important? Because it works! We've already talked about how being mindful can help you learn to identify and regulate your emotions and enhance your connection with your child. But there are many other reasons to practice mindfulness.

Benefits of Mindfulness

So many people practice mindfulness because:

- **It reduces stress levels.** Mindfulness has been proven to help you sleep. And we all know it's easier to deal with a toddler who refuses to wear a shirt when we've had eight hours of sleep instead of two.
- **It lowers anxiety.** Mindfulness can alleviate anxiety, so you can worry less about your child, your parenting, and yourself.
- **It combats depression.** Mindfulness can help you stay in the present moment while also helping you break away from negative thoughts.
- **It can stop disruptive behaviors.** Mindfulness can make it easier for parents to be more aware of their feelings. With lowered blood pressure, parents can react to problems the way they want to instead of lashing out.

When you're being mindful, you're not focused on juggling the million and a half things that you're responsible for as a parent. Instead, you're focused on the present moment. One of the long-term advantages of using mindfulness is that you don't miss out on the relationship between you and your child.

We've all heard that children grow up so fast. It's true. You don't want to get to your kid's high school graduation and realize that you were so focused on making sure they never had a failing grade that you missed actually developing a true connection with them. If you need a reason to turn to mindful parenting, do it for the long-lasting bond. Do it so you can begin to appreciate that Friday night ice cream run together or that after-dinner bicycle ride around the neighborhood. When you begin to appreciate those little moments while you're experiencing them, you can communicate more openly with your child.

According to the Gottman Institute, there are three important things parents do when parenting mindfully. The first is **noticing how they're feeling** when they're having a problem with their child. The second is **pausing before responding or disengaging** from the situation. The third essential thing that mindful parents do is **listen to their child**, even if their kid is saying something they disagree with.

Let's look at another example of mindful parenting in action. Imagine that your son repeatedly comes home from school and puts off doing his homework for hours. Every day, it's a battle to get him to complete it. Your current "strategy" for dealing with this is to yell through his bedroom door, "You'd better be doing your homework in there."

A more mindful parenting approach would be to take a moment to disengage from the situation. Ask yourself, *How can I help him?* Opening a line of communication with him (one where you're talking rather than yelling) is a great start. Start by asking what he needs to feel comfortable and focused.

You may be surprised when he says his teacher always plays classical music during math class, and he's having a hard time focusing without music. In this case, it's a simple solution to play some music on the radio or your phone.

He might instead say he's too tired to start on his homework right after the school day ends. In this situation, why not let him lay down for a half-hour of rest every day from 3:00 to 3:30 pm? Then, at 3:30 pm, he gets a quick snack to re-energize and start his homework at 3:45 pm. You may be shifting your schedule just a little, but the payoff will be worth it.

Besides, in the end, you'll actually save time since you won't be yelling and micromanaging for hours.

STRATEGIES FOR CENTERING YOURSELF

Once you start looking for strategies to calm yourself and refocus your mind, you'll be amazed at how many are out there. Ask your friends with similarly aged children how they deal with certain behaviors. They may have a nice trick up their sleeve that you never knew would work. Chances are, you'll also have a parenting hack you can give them in return.

Throughout the generations, parents have bonded together to find ways to get through those tough parenting challenges. Don't be afraid to ask your child's daycare teacher, school teacher, or coach for tips on keeping your cool. These individuals have worked with tons of children and have a wealth of knowledge for dealing with tricky situations. More importantly, they've worked with *your* child. There may be a special strategy they've used to get your kid out of a funk.

Here's what centering strategies can look like:

1. **Find your physical center.** Centering yourself isn't just a mental practice. It's just as much a physical one, which means identifying your own "center" is essential. Think back to when you were last so angry you felt the emotion overwhelming your body. Your breath was likely short and shallow, and your lungs were working overtime to keep your breathing in check. When you center yourself, you can imagine your breath coming from that area about two inches below your navel (sometimes referred to as the *dantian* or hypogastrium).
2. **Do a full-body scan.** Consider your body at the moment. While you may feel relatively at peace while reading this book, you likely have tight muscles somewhere. In a way, you may be holding your stress and frustration in these parts. For example, many people clench their jaws throughout the day. Is your jaw completely relaxed? Maybe your brow is slightly furrowed, and you didn't realize it until just now. Take a moment to perform a full-body scan, starting from the crown of your head and working down to your toes. Focus on relaxing every muscle in your body. You may find it helpful to visualize a relaxing, positive energy radiating throughout your body as you do so.
3. **Mentally release negative energy.** I understand how hard it can be to let go of those nagging, annoying thoughts that irritate you. When we feel upset, we tend to hold that tension within us. Instead, imagine you are using all those unhappy thoughts to form a

ball of energy. Let every negative thought come to mind, and pretend each one is added to the energy ball. Once you have every last thought in the ball, pretend to throw it out the window. Feels pretty good, doesn't it?

4. **Try a quick yoga routine.** While some yoga classes are designed to give you an intense workout, not all of them are. In fact, many are intended to help you relax and find peace in the moment. There are a ton of yoga positions to choose from, and you can even develop your own "calm-me-down flow" for those tougher moments.

5. **Practice deep breathing exercises.** Breathing deeply is something you can do anytime, anywhere. When you're feeling stressed and need to find your inner calm, take a seat, lie down, or even stand up. Close your eyes if that feels comfortable or look down at a spot on the floor with unfocused eyes (that's where you're "seeing" but not really noticing what you're looking at). Breathe in, filling your lungs, and then exhale slowly. Concentrate on your breath the entire time. Notice how it inflates your lungs and then deflates them.

Now, it's time to put these centering strategies into action! It's one thing to have your mental toolbox filled with all these aids, but it's a whole different process to actually put them to use.

Let's walk through a hypothetical day of mindfully parenting your seven-year-old. It's time to wake your daughter up for breakfast. In the past, your child has had a hard time getting out of bed, which becomes a struggle, especially on school days. Today, you gently wake her up and talk to her in a soothing tone. You turn on her favorite "wake-up song" that she requested. Soon, she is smiling and jumping out of bed.

She comes to the breakfast table. She's upset that you all are eating cereal when you said last night you would make pancakes for breakfast. You take a moment to yourself at the stove as you feel anger starting to well up. Instead of snapping that she should be happy to have food on the table, you close your eyes for a few seconds.

You take a deep breath and focus on your center. Now, you realize that your daughter is only disappointed and confused. You tell her, "I was hoping we could have pancakes, too. But we were out of eggs when I looked in the refrigerator." (You *don't* add: "Because your father/mother forgot to pick them up from the store yesterday . . . again!") Instead, you tell your kid, "When we go to the grocery store later today, we'll pick up more eggs so we can have pancakes tomorrow."

Later that afternoon, you work in a yoga session in preparation for going to the grocery store. You know you have a busy schedule, but you prioritize devoting fifteen minutes to your physical and mental well-being. While your daughter is getting dressed, you do your calm-me-down yoga routine: a few rounds of child's pose, sun salutations, and cat-cow poses.

Once in the car, the ride is fairly calm because you remembered to bring the car activity bag for her. This bag is one your daughter helped fill. It contains a book she likes, a fidget toy, a magnetic drawing board, and a little toy car that looks like the family car. She likes playing with it in the car because it's something she and you made together so that she doesn't feel so bored on car rides.

At the grocery store, you give her a special shopping list so she can help get some items, too. She enjoys hunting for the special food. While finding the items on her list, she sees some candy she wants, but she already has a lot at home. She starts to scream that she wants the candy. Before you respond, you realize you're getting embarrassed and angry. You remember to take a moment to disengage before correcting her behavior. You do a quick body scan, making sure your muscles are all relaxed, and you're not responding in anger.

Once you've recentered yourself, you tell your daughter calmly, "You already have candy at home. Your tantrum is disrupting the other shoppers. You can write down the candy name on your list for next time, but we are not getting it today." As she continues to whine for a few minutes, you ignore her, and within two or three minutes, she forgets about the candy and is back to her list.

When you get home, you put away the groceries while your daughter plays with her toys. As you start cooking dinner, she tells you she's bored. It's tempting to put on the television for her, but you think about how your partner has been working extra hours this week, and your daughter is on a school break. So there's a good chance she's a little lonely.

You ask if she would like to help you mix the biscuit dough in a bowl. She happily agrees, and you get to share a few minutes of cooking together. At this moment, you remember how much you enjoyed cooking with your family when you were little. Cooking with your daughter makes you happy, too, since you get to create a similar memory for her.

That night, as your partner is getting your daughter ready for bed, you spend a few minutes meditating. You set a timer on your phone so that everyone knows not to disturb you for fifteen minutes. By the time you're ready to sleep yourself, you feel relaxed and content.

You may have some days where mindful parenting seems to come easily and others when you must remind yourself to center yourself repeatedly. Consider starting your day off with a mindful practice of your choosing each and every day. This way, the process will get easier over time.

Keep a list of your centering strategies in your wallet. Make a collage or vision board that symbolizes your favorite ways to relax. Refer to these items whenever you need to disengage from a potentially stressful situation.

CALMING ACTIVITY BINGO SHEET

The more strategies you try, the more likely it is that you will find some that work really well for you and your family. Remember, when your children (and your partner!) see you taking steps to center yourself, they'll begin to adopt these strategies, too. When you're doing yoga, your child will almost certainly want to try it out. By caring for yourself, you're also introducing your child to a variety of techniques that will help them in life.

You may be learning about these strategies later in life, but imagine if you had learned emotional regulation and centering techniques from early childhood. You may have had a very different experience growing up!

Here is a Calming Activity Bingo Sheet that you can use when you're feeling stressed out. Try to get a Bingo by doing several in a row!

Breathe deeply for two minutes	Journal	Bake your favorite cookies and enjoy the experience	Go for a swim	Spend time with a pet
Do a yoga sequence	Listen to your favorite song	Make a cup of tea	Take a bubble bath	Count down from 10
Go for a jog	Create an affirmation to repeat each day	Free Space	Light a candle	Visualize throwing away a ball of negative thoughts
Schedule time to sit with your emotions	Meditate for five minutes	Color an adult coloring book page	Go for a walk in nature	Schedule a coffee date with a friend
Do a full-body scan	Read your favorite book	Listen to a calming podcast	Do a couple of stretches	Create a vision board of relaxation methods

Now that you're (hopefully) feeling more confident in your ability to bring peace and calm into your life, we'll move on to the next chapter, where I'll share some of my favorite strategies for preventing anger in the first place.

Chapter Takeaways:

- Mindful parenting means responding to your child's behavior with love and deep consideration.
- Try out several centering strategies so you can discover which ones work for you.
- Remind yourself often of strategies that are available to you. Incorporate them into your daily routine.

6

EFFECTIVE STRATEGIES FOR ANGER PREVENTION

"The greatest weapon against stress is our ability to choose one thought over another."

— WILLIAM JAMES

All too frequently, parents let minor, daily stressors accumulate. Eventually, there's a breaking point as to how much stress you can contain, and the result is often explosive anger. Have you and your partner ever gotten into an argument, but you find yourself getting upset with your child instead?

Maybe you've been dealing with chronic migraines, and it seems like every time you get one, your kid is getting on your last nerve. If any of these situations sound like you, there's a good chance you're not healthily dealing with your stress. The stress-anger link is real, and it's up to you to regulate your stress.

In Chapter 6, I'll discuss some ways you can keep your cool when you're beginning to feel that familiar tug of stress. Some of these methods involve preventing stress in the first place (and subsequently, preventing anger). Others will help you deal with stress in the moment because, sometimes, you won't be able to prevent feeling overwhelmed.

EXPLORING THE LINK BETWEEN STRESS AND ANGER IN PARENTING

What stresses me may not stress you and vice-versa. Both of our children can break a window in our house, but one of us may laugh it off while the other stresses about the cost and repair time.

It is up to you to take a deep, introspective look to identify your short-term and long-term stressors. Here are some examples of situations that can make you feel stressed for a short period of time:

- **Brief sickness.** You may have a cold, the flu, or strep throat. These illnesses are typically fleeting and are resolved within a week or two.
- **Temporary work stress.** Maybe you have a big project you're trying to complete by the end of the week.
- **Family illness.** If your own mother or father is having surgery or is recovering from an accident, you might feel stressed until they've recouped.

- **Financial problems.** Have you ever had your car break down just after you've paid it off? Not a fun feeling.
- **Traffic.** Getting stuck in rush hour traffic is never enjoyable. You may find your blood pressure elevating while in a bumper-to-bumper traffic jam.
- **Worry.** When you're worried about something like a fraudulent charge on your credit card or getting your child's paperwork in by a deadline so they can start kindergarten, you might be a little more on edge.

This list is not exhaustive, of course. Life seems to throw stress our way in more ways than we can count. While short-term stress goes away after some time and can be more easily avoided, long-term stress sticks around.

When you're dealing with a chronic illness, recurrent financial hardship, a long daily commute, or perpetual caregiving for a family member, you face long-term stress. Since there's no end to these situations in sight, you'll have to learn to deal with the inevitable stress that comes with them.

Ways You Can Manage Your Stress

Keeping stress levels to a minimum is the ideal coping strategy. After all, isn't it easier to prevent a fire than try to get it under control once it's raging? Take a moment to think about ways you can eliminate your common stress triggers.

Can you take the slightly longer but more scenic (and less crowded) route to and from work each day? Maybe you can adjust your schedule by half an hour to avoid peak rush hour times. This way, when you get home, you can greet your child with a smile and a joke instead of a tired sigh.

If your stress comes from financial uncertainty, this can be a bit tougher to resolve. Applying to higher-paying jobs may help. Picking up some part-time work, like babysitting your neighbor's kids, could be a low-stress option that brings in additional money. Asking for help from family members or friends could also alleviate stress. Maybe your in-laws have offered to buy your kid's back-to-school clothes. Why not let them?

Avoiding substances like sugar, nicotine, and caffeine (found in tea, coffee, and chocolate) can also prevent stress. These everyday items are known for contributing to stress and anger. Avoiding that third cup of coffee or that late-night chocolate binge may help you feel more at ease throughout the day. While quitting nicotine may feel incredibly stressful at the time, the long-term benefits to your health, mood, and wallet can eliminate future stress.

Other things, like engaging in your favorite hobbies and exercising, can also lower your stress. Sign up for a gym membership and prioritize that time. If you go to a barre or weightlifting class every Monday at 5:30 pm, you'll have dedicated time to work out that stress.

You can also try to plan around your stress. For example, you can take a few minutes at the beginning of the day to consider what might cause stress in the morning, afternoon, or evening. You might pinpoint getting your child to brush their teeth after they wake up to be a stressful time, mostly because they take forever and are sometimes late for school. You may also note your 10 am meeting at work to be a recurring stressor. Later, trying to get all the household chores finished by bedtime is another strain.

Once you have a detailed list of all your expected stressors, you can go ahead and get an action plan in place. You can schedule an extra fifteen minutes for toothbrushing. This way, you're not so pressured to rush your child through the process, and you're less likely to be late dropping them off.

For that 10 am meeting, you can make yourself a calming cup of your favorite tea blend to take into the meeting. You can also plan on doing a ten-second count mentally at the beginning of the meeting. This will help you center yourself and keep your stress at bay.

To combat the stress you're feeling about the household chores, you can ask your partner to take over dinner duty. You can also plan to pop a load of laundry in the washer while helping your child with their homework.

Sometimes, the best way to deal with stress is to get help by talking with folks outside your immediate circle. You may seek professional help, which can take the form of counseling or therapy. In this case, a trained counselor or therapist can work with you to identify areas to work on. You may also choose to join a stress support group. Speaking with your peers (including other parents) about their stress management tactics can help you feel supported.

Of course, you should also lean on your partner, if you're raising your child together. You may think your partner doesn't experience stress because they appear so calm and collected, but that likely means they have developed their own stress management tricks. Don't assume your partner intuitively knows you are having a hard time controlling your stress. It can seem so evident to you that you're overwhelmed by work, childcare, and bills, but your partner may not have picked up on your signals.

You can also talk to your friends and family. Seek out those people you admire for their emotional control. Who are those people who seem constantly at peace? Most people will be happy to share their relaxing strategies. Supportive friends and family will want to help you lower your stress levels. If they're not interested in helping, they may very well be a source of stress themselves.

THE IMPACT OF SELF-CARE ON ANGER MANAGEMENT

In an earlier chapter, we discussed the physical effects of long-term stress and anger. If you allow these problems to continue unchecked, you may begin to suffer physical and emotional consequences. Stress and anger feed on each other, and it's not uncommon to find yourself in a difficult-to-break cycle.

Self-care can help stop the constant stress. Self-care is a term we hear tossed around frequently, but it's easy to forget what it means. When you're practicing self-care, you are nourishing (caring for) yourself just as you do for the people around you. As parents, we spend so much of our day ensuring our children have everything they need.

It's just as important to take a step back and remember that we must give ourselves the essentials too. That means devoting time to relaxing, sleeping, exercising, and sometimes, just enjoying the silence! If your household is like many, there are few moments of complete quiet in the day.

Giving yourself a break from the chaos and pampering yourself can heal some of your stress while getting you in a good mindset for the rest of the day.

When you care for yourself, you have the energy, both physical and mental, to take care of those around you. It's one of those paradoxical things where you have to invest some time upfront to get the payoff later.

Consider the life of a busy father who doesn't do self-care. He went to bed late the night before and wakes up in a rush. He skips breakfast because he wants to make sure his children all get to school on time. He grabs fast food on his lunch break because he's juggling household errands. Maybe he's coming down with a cold, but he refuses to take a day off work because he doesn't want to disappoint his boss. At home, he spends his remaining energy keeping the house immaculate. By the time he hits the bed, he is exhausted. The cycle continues the next day.

It doesn't take much imagination to realize this kind of lifestyle isn't very sustainable. It may work for him in the short term, but eventually, he will get burned out. Skipping meals and eating fast food all the time will make him feel sluggish and possibly lead to health complications.

How can this dad incorporate self-care into his routine?

First, he can prioritize eating breakfast in the morning. He notices when he sits down and eats a bowl of granola, he feels more energized. His children like that he sits and shares a meal with them. (Believe it or not, they care more about this than whether their clothes match perfectly!) This dad can also start packing a healthy lunch like a whole grain sandwich and fresh fruit and vegetables.

While taking a few extra minutes to pack lunch means he won't have as much time to scroll through social media or check his work email in the morning, he realizes spending time focused on his health is more important.

This father can also practice self-care by taking a day off work when he needs it. He can accept that he's sick and that he, just like his child, needs time to heal. When it comes to the neverending pile of housework that waits for him at home, he devotes just one hour a night to household chores. He sets a timer, and when it goes off, he spends the rest of the night hanging out with his kids or doing something he genuinely enjoys, like reading. He makes sure to get into bed at a decent time every night so he wakes up refreshed.

Self-care can feel a little selfish at first if you're not used to taking care of yourself. You're probably thinking, "Wait? It's okay if I put on my mud mask instead of folding my kids' laundry? That can't be right." You might think something as simple as making time for your favorite skin care regimen is silly. But the truth is, these small pleasures are ways of self-soothing. If you've had a long day at work and with the kids, indulging in your organic avocado-honey-lavender mud mask might be the difference between snapping at your child and feeling guilty or handling conflict smoothly and appropriately.

Self-care can have major impacts on mental health. In fact, the practice can be used to help deal with depression and anxiety. When you consider all the areas self-care can support, it's not surprising that this strategy brings about results.

Five major types of self-care serve to improve your life. These include:

1. Mental

Have you ever worked a job that you found menial and repetitive? You were probably bored out of your mind, and that's because you weren't mentally stimulated. If you spend most of your time doing activities that don't engage you, you'll likely feel "off." Mental self-care means caring for that intellectual part of yourself. Mental self-care activities can include reading books, taking courses, and listening to podcasts that speak to your life passions.

2. Spiritual

When you practice spiritual self-care, you're nourishing your soul. For some people, this can be going to church, synagogue, mosque, or other religious institutions. However, even nonreligious people must take care of their spiritual needs. You can set aside time to consider your life's purpose, meditate, or spend time in nature.

3. Emotional

Caring for yourself emotionally is essential if you're serious about managing your anger. Some things you can do to take care of your emotional health include scheduling alone time. Take a day for yourself and spend some time without work or home commitments. You can also watch movies that make you feel especially happy, or, if you need a good cry (don't we all sometimes?), you can put on your favorite tearjerker.

4. Physical

In our fast-paced world, physical self-care is getting harder and harder to achieve. When we care for our bodies, though, we are investing in our long-term health. Go out for a run or take a spin class at the local gym. Caring for your physical health can even be accomplished through slower-paced activities like a walk in the park. Choosing nutritious meals that you take your time to eat can also help you slow down and respect your body. Ensuring you get sufficient sleep each night (typically seven to eight hours) is another way to care for your physical being.

5. Social

Sometimes, we need other people to help us care for ourselves. Even if you're the biggest introvert you know, you still need some form of social interaction with others. Feed your social needs by making time to chat with friends over the phone, on video chat, or in person. Schedule a lunch date or head to the movies for a grown-up, nonanimated movie. (Seriously, when was the last time you watched a movie that didn't involve cartoon characters?)

SELF-CARE WORKSHEET

In the chaos of the day, it's easy to put self-care on the back burner. Remember that caring for yourself is just as important as caring for others. As the saying goes, you can't refill someone else's bucket with an empty one. In other words, you must care for yourself first to be in a good state to care for someone else.

Use this worksheet to help you develop your self-care strategy for the coming months.

1. **Use your calendar.** Open your calendar or planner, and identify time for self-care. You've probably scheduled your child's soccer practice, so why not your self-care sessions? Honor the time you block off just as you would for a work obligation.
2. **Set self-care goals.** Think about why you want to care for yourself. Is it so you have more energy and happiness to spread to your children? Is it so you can feel ready to take on the day or accomplish work and home goals? Write out your self-care goals and commit to them.
3. **Stick to healthy activities.** It can be tempting to think of binging on cake as a prime example of self-care, but consider whether your actions are ultimately in your best interest. Focus on doing things that give you long-term gratification instead of small, momentary (and unhealthy) boosts like those from cigarettes or alcohol.
4. **Keep it up.** Once you start caring for yourself, it will begin to get easier. Your friends and family will come to know that Wednesdays are your day for caring for yourself. Once self-care becomes a habit, you'll have an easier time saying "No" to people when they want to schedule over your personal spa day, for example.

5. **Do things you actually enjoy.** Have you committed to training for a marathon only to realize you hate running? Self-care isn't about doing activities that you think others find helpful. Instead, focus on activities that you truly enjoy. That might be something as far-fetched as unicycling or as mundane as rock collecting.
6. **Revisit your self-care plan regularly.** Over time, your self-care needs may change. For example, if you begin a new job where you're on your feet all day, your physical self-care activities may need to become more sedentary, like stretching. Similarly, if your recent routine includes doing a lot of number crunching, you may nourish your mental needs by watching a mindless television show instead of reading.

Whenever you feel yourself slipping in your self-care routine, remember why you committed to doing it in the first place. Self-care is a way to disengage from your anger. The practice can help you stay calm around your child. You'll then be ready to reengage with them peacefully.

Sounds pretty nice, doesn't it? In the next chapter, I'll show you how!

Chapter Takeaways:

- Unmanaged stress can lead to anger.
- Prevent stressful situations when possible. Manage unavoidable stress through relaxing activities.
- There are five types of self-care (mental, spiritual, emotional, physical, and social). Each is important for maintaining balance in your life.

YOU'RE NOT THE ONLY ONE

"Where there is anger, there is always pain underneath."

— ECKHART TOLLE

You've probably seen the odd parent at the school gate who you're fairly sure struggles with their anger just as much as you do. They're the ones who aren't so good at hiding it – the ones who openly scream at their kids because they're late or refusing to listen when it's time to stop playing. But there are more parents than you realize who are struggling too – they're the ones who might be more like you, rarely being pushed to the breaking point in public, but facing battles with their anger at home on a daily basis.

We've all been there, and that's why building these strategies is so important. Often, you feel like you're the only one, but this issue affects more parents than you realize. That tense feeling you get when you have to fight to keep your anger under control can be overwhelming, and the guilt that comes with it is heavy. You shouldn't have to feel like that...*No one* should have to feel like that. And that's the reason this book exists.

As a parent who's working hard to overcome the same struggles, I know you understand, so I'd like to take this opportunity to ask for your help in reaching more parents.

By leaving a review of this book on Amazon, you'll show other parents who want to get their anger under control where they can find all the help they need to succeed.

Simply by letting new readers know how this book has helped you and what they'll find inside, you'll be doing two important things: You'll be showing them that they're not alone, and you'll be guiding them toward the strategies that will help them break the cycle.

Thank you so much for your support. The guilt that comes with not being able to manage our anger as parents is terrible… Together, we can help more people break free.

Scan the QR code to leave a review!

STEP 3: RE-ENGAGE WITH YOUR CHILD

7

STRENGTHENING BONDS AND RECONNECTING WITH YOUR CHILD

> *"Like a trained surgeon who is careful where he cuts, parents, too, need to become skilled in the use of words. Because words are like knives. They can inflict, if not physical, many painful emotional wounds."*
>
> — HAIM G. GINOTT, BETWEEN PARENT AND CHILD: REVISED AND UPDATED: THE BESTSELLING CLASSIC THAT REVOLUTIONIZED PARENT-CHILD COMMUNICATION

How do you feel when you think about those parenting moments you regret, such as when you threw away your child's favorite toy in anger or didn't let them attend that birthday party because you were upset with them? If you're like many parents, you may feel repairing your relationship after these moments is impossible.

Don't stress because your relationship can still be salvaged. Up until now, I've shared a lot of information about acknowledging your anger and then disengaging from it. Now, you're ready to re-engage with your child and let them know things are going to be different moving forward. With some effort on your part, you can begin to strengthen the bond you share with your child.

In Chapter 7, I will show you how you can begin a conversation about anger and problem-solving with them. You'll learn some key communication tips to ensure you and your child feel respected and listened to during these discussions.

DISCUSSING ANGER AND FINDING SOLUTIONS TOGETHER

In that fruitless quest to become the perfect parent, you may feel like you're never supposed to be angry. Don't forget that moderate anger, in certain situations, can be useful. When your child sees you angry on occasion, they will understand that something has made you unhappy. So keep in mind that it's okay for your kid to know you're angry! There's just a huge difference between volatile anger that leads you to shout at your child and controlled anger that you communicate appropriately.

Those times when you're experiencing managed anger are ideal for communicating with your child. Once you've taken a moment to disengage from the situation and find your cool, you can open a line of communication with your child.

Let's take a moment to explore what sort of things you should and shouldn't do and say as you begin to discuss your anger.

Do:

- Speak about your own emotions using "I" statements. ("I feel frustrated when I feel like my words are not being heard.")
- Explain why you're angry. ("I'm angry because I asked you to clean your room, but your toys are still out.)
- Discuss what are appropriate ways of showing anger. ("Talking about anger is a good way to communicate. Hitting is not.")
- Problem-solve with your child. ("Let's talk about why you didn't pick up your toys and what we can do about it.")

Don't:

- Verbally attack your child. ("You never listen to me!")
- Pretend you don't feel emotions. ("I'm not mad. Why would I be mad?")
- Hit your child.
- Create a solution all on your own. ("This is how we're going to do it.")

When we talk about anger with our kids in a calm, loving way, we're not condoning their actions. We're still expressing our unhappiness with the situation, but we're doing it in a way that makes our children feel safe and heard.

Think about it this way. If your partner came up to you and started shouting, "You always do this! You never take out the trash! Why won't you listen?" you'd probably tune them out pretty quickly. Instead of listening, you'd be worrying about their next move.

The same goes for your child. Try saying, "Let's talk about why I'm feeling mad right now. I'd love for you to help find a way to fix this situation," instead of, "You're making me so mad right now. You'd better clean up this mess, or you won't like what happens next!"

Your kids need to be reminded that you're human too. As a parent, your children automatically think you're a superhero with all the solutions. It's okay to let them know you make mistakes just like they do. Share some of those stories from when you were a child. Like that time you stole your parents' wallet and spent $20 at the ice cream truck. Or the time you dyed the dog blue with food coloring.

Talking about your current and former mistakes shows your child it's okay to talk about their feelings. When they see you learning from your mistakes, this sets a fantastic model for your child. They'll begin to acknowledge their own emotions and actions.

Making communication a family event can give everyone a sense of responsibility when it comes to regulating their emotions. Whether it's you, your partner, or one of your children, everyone will feel like they can verbalize their feelings instead of acting out in anger. As you might expect, this can create a much more harmonious environment.

Yes, your family can be that family on TV who sits down in the living room and discusses what's on their mind (think *Full House* style). While you may think it's a bit cheesy, consider how much nicer it is to talk about your feelings instead of throwing things and yelling (more *Real Housewives* style).

RECONNECTING WITH YOUR CHILD AFTER A CONFLICT

After a major blow-up, do you feel tension in the air at your house? Your child may be walking on eggshells around you. After a few days, things get back to normal, right? Wrong. It may seem like your child has forgotten all about your angry episode, but they haven't. Kids bottle up those memories and carry them into adulthood (and then dissect them with their therapists).

Before those memories get sealed shut, add a bit more substance to the memory. You may have lost your temper in the past, but that doesn't mean you can't apologize to your kid today. For some reason, our society steers away from apologizing to children, but it's a healthy and loving way to bond with your child.

When you do apologize, make sure your apology is effective. Don't try to get around it by saying things like, "Sorry you were such a little terror this morning. You made me mad." Instead, you can form a thoughtful apology by saying something like, "I'm sorry I yelled the way I did earlier. You don't deserve to be shouted at like that. The next time I get angry, I will take a few minutes to cool down before we talk about things."

Leave out those "buts" and "ifs." That means an apology that starts out with something like, "I'm sorry I got so mad, but you . . ." is not a true apology. Take responsibility for your anger. Other important elements that comprise a real apology include explaining (truthfully) why you were upset, considering how your child felt at the time, showing empathy for them, and being remorseful.

But communication isn't just about talking. It's also about listening. Encourage your child to talk with you about their feelings and thoughts and listen attentively. At this point, you may be worried about what your child is going to say. If you've been doing a lot of shouting over the years, it's your turn to listen.

Before you freak out at the thought of hearing your child say exactly what they think of you and your anger, take a deep breath. Consider this conversation as an answer key to a test. All this time, you've been wondering why your child "won't listen," and they're about to tell you what's been going on. It's a good thing, I promise.

If you're not sure how to break the ice, I have some ideas for you:

- "How can I help you at this moment?"
- "What can I do to help you feel loved?"
- "How about we start over?"
- "Is it okay if I give you a hug?"
- "How are you feeling right now?"

Don't shy away from apologizing and communicating with your partner, either. Your actions have probably affected them just as much as your child. Strengthening the relationship between you and your partner can indirectly help your child too. Your kid will see how their parents discuss problems in a peaceful, loving manner.

IMPORTANCE OF EFFECTIVE COMMUNICATION IN ANGER MANAGEMENT

Four types of communication styles exist, including passive, aggressive, passive-aggressive, and assertive. Someone who communicates passively may be opposed to making decisions and has a hard time letting others know what they want or need. Aggressive communicators have the opposite issue. They are very firm and demanding when it comes to expressing their opinions. As parents, they may often shout and make strict demands of their children.

Passive-aggressive communication combines these two types. As the term suggests, the communicator is aggressive in their communication but does so in a passive way. For instance, a passive-aggressive parent may relay their unhappiness with their child's behavior by giving them the cold shoulder instead of talking to them rationally.

Assertive communication is the best style to use when talking with your child. Why? Because people who use this type of communication clearly convey their needs and thoughts but do it respectfully and appropriately. It can take some practice to get used to communicating assertively, but it will get easier the more you work at it.

Let's examine the different ways a parent could communicate their unhappiness. In this example, a parent is angry that their child has been skipping school.

Passive: (sarcastically) "Oh, right. You didn't feel like going to school, did you?"

Aggressive: "You didn't go to school because you're lazy."

Passive-aggressive: (under their breath) "You might be going out tonight if you hadn't skipped school last week."

Assertive: "It's important you go to school so you don't fall behind. It's difficult to catch up once you've missed so much school."

If you're used to communicating not quite so effectively, there are things you can do to improve your assertive communication skills. You can stop yourself from jumping to conclusions and making assumptions. For instance, you might be tempted to assume your child skipped school because they don't feel like doing schoolwork. But once you start talking with them, you may learn that they're feeling embarrassed because the teacher calls on them when they don't know the answer to a question.

You can also listen to your child as they explain their side of the story. Truly listen to what they're saying. Ask more questions. Why are they embarrassed that they don't know the answer? Has something happened previously to make them think the class will laugh at them?

When you're communicating assertively, be clear about your feelings. As we've discussed, it's okay to tell your child you're angry that they've been skipping school. But you can also tell them this anger came from fear of not knowing where they were for an afternoon. You might also be worried they'll get held back a year and lose touch with their friends.

STRATEGIES FOR ACTIVE LISTENING AND ASSERTIVE EXPRESSION

Have you ever been talking with someone about something really exciting, but you notice their eyes start to glaze over? And when they respond, their answers are short and dismissive, like "Oh, okay. That's nice."

Realizing someone's not listening to you isn't a good feeling, especially when you are eager to share news with them. When we're not listened to, we may feel rejected, embarrassed, or even angry. Your child will feel the same when they don't feel heard, and this can lead to disruptive behaviors and misunderstanding.

Communication is much more pleasant and effective when both parties are actively listening. When a person is actively listening, it means they are engaged in the listening process. Not only are they hearing what the other person is saying, but they're also letting the talker know that they understand what they're communicating.

When someone is listening actively, they often maintain eye contact to show they are following along. (Note that some cultures show respect by avoiding eye contact.) Another way to demonstrate you are giving a speaker your full attention is to paraphrase what they're saying (Ex. "So you went to the library, and they didn't have the book you wanted?"). You can also give nonverbal cues that you're listening attentively by nodding your head.

Another way to demonstrate you're engaged is to ask follow-up questions about the story or comment on certain parts of it. Showing the person you're putting mental energy into listening can make them feel good and appreciated.

Incorporating active listening into your family discussions is a wonderful way to make everyone feel heard and respected. Both you and your child can practice this skill to make expressing your emotions easier. One way you can do this is by role-playing a scenario. You can take turns telling each other about your day.

Child: This morning, I woke up, and I got on the school bus. Then, I went to science class, and we made really cool slime with glitter.

Parent: Ooh, I bet that was fun. You love slime!

Child: Yeah, I brought some home to show you. But after we made slime, we went to math class which was kind of boring.

Parent: [nods]

Child: Then, in history, we played a game where we could pretend to be people from the Medieval Ages. For lunch, we had pizza, but they put on olives, so I didn't like it. I didn't eat much of it. Then, we played kickball in gym, and I came home.

Parent: You didn't eat lunch and then played kickball? You're probably starving!

Take a turn talking to your kid about your day. Ask them to comment on certain things so you know they've heard you. You can get goofy with it and make up funny stories. The point right now is to simply practice those active listening skills.

You might even be surprised to learn that active listening can be a form of mindfulness. When you're focused on listening attentively, your mind is not wandering. You are present in the moment, and your only focus is your child.

So put away your phone, put the computer in sleep mode, and turn off the TV for a few minutes. Spend some quality time talking with your child and getting to know them a little better! Practicing this skill during fun, lighthearted times will make it easier to have those more difficult discussions.

MANAGING CONFLICT IN A HEALTHY WAY

If you're like many people, you cringe at the idea of conflict. You might get extremely rattled when your child or someone else does something you don't like. This conflict aversion may lead you to act passively (avoid the situation altogether), aggressively (shout about it), or passive-aggressively (secretly stew on it).

But those old, unhelpful communication styles are a thing of the past, at least for you. Now, you're a parent working on their assertive communication methods! Let's dive into ways you can manage conflict effectively.

Perhaps one of the biggest struggles is accepting that conflict is going to happen. Even if you follow a gentle parenting approach, practice self-care, and regulate your emotions, you and your child will butt heads. It's part of life. Your child will push boundaries by nature. They're still learning how the world works and how to be a human in it. Come to think of it, so are you! Just because you're older doesn't mean you aren't still learning too.

Break down the conflict. Study it, and learn from it. What are the events that led your daughter to yell at you from the school parking lot? Was it because you scolded her in front of her friends, and she got embarrassed? Did she have a bad day at school and took it out on you? Were you short with her because *you* had a rough workday? The more you learn about the situation, the easier it is to identify what went wrong and how you can prevent it from happening again.

When you're managing a conflict with your child, remember to consult them when finding a solution. We've discussed how important it is to make your kid feel like they have agency in the relationship. When it comes to conflict resolution, be open to their thoughts. Your daughter may explain she yelled because you embarrassed her in front of her crush. Next time, you won't publicly remind her to take her acne medicine.

If you've been speaking to your child about a mistake they made, respect their privacy. The other kids in the household don't need to know all the details. Parents who grew up in a multi-child household will surely remember the teasing you got when you got in trouble! When you respectfully discuss a conflict with your child one-on-one, they'll be more willing to listen and less focused on what their siblings are overhearing.

Sometimes, our child has a hard time talking about conflict. They may be unsure why they're behaving the way they are. In this case, you can help them brainstorm some reasons why they might be upset.

Your son might be struggling to deal with the birth of a new sibling. The change in schedule, noise level, and dynamic of your home could have upset him. For a very young child, these changes can be hard to identify, but they can certainly make him angry.

Other significant transitions, like starting kindergarten or another new grade, can stress out your child. As you know by now, stress can lead to angry outbursts and irritability. Some additional things to consider are a friend moving away, a new teacher at school, problems sleeping, and physical problems.

As a parent, you have the perfect opportunity to practice your active listening skills in this kind of scenario. Listen intently to the clues your kid provides about what might be triggering conflict.

ACTIVE LISTENING AND CONFLICT RESOLUTION WORKSHEET

Here's a cheat sheet for when you're working on resolving a conflict but can't figure out where to start.

1. **Analyze the conflict.** What exactly happened? Try to get as much information about the conflict as possible.
2. **Be the first person to apologize.** You may want to dig in your heels, but step up and be a responsible parent. Apologize to your child effectively. Remember, that means no qualifiers, i.e., "I wouldn't have gotten mad if you hadn't put the fork in the toaster."

3. **Admit that you're angry.** Be honest with your child and tell them why you were mad. Just do so in a polite, respectful tone.
4. **Invite your child to communicate.** Ask your child to tell you their side of the story. Let them know you are eager to hear their thoughts and to understand what happened.
5. **Practice active listening.** As your child talks, make sure you're giving them your full attention. Don't answer work calls or scroll through your phone as they talk.
6. **Find solutions together.** Share your ideas for preventing conflict in the future.

Once you've mastered the art of reconnecting with your child, you can help them build additional communication skills. In the following chapter, I will break down what this looks like for each age group.

Chapter Takeaways:

- Once you learn to regulate your anger, you can begin repairing your relationship with your child.
- Use effective apologies to open a line of communication with your family. Find solutions together.
- Practice active listening when communicating with your child. Teach them how to actively listen when you are talking.

8

SPEAK THEIR LANGUAGE: COMMUNICATION SKILLS FOR EVERY AGE

"Love is the supreme form of communication. In the hierarchy of needs, love stands as the supreme developing agent of the humanity of the person. As such, the teaching of love should be the central core of all early childhood curriculum with all other subjects growing naturally out of such teaching."

— ASHLEY MONTAGU

We've been talking a lot about how important communicating with our children is. As we've learned, healthy communication sets expectations and prevents misunderstandings. When parents verbalize their emotions and provide clear rules and boundaries, anger management becomes much easier.

But when speaking with kids, there isn't a one-size-fits-all approach.

Depending on your child's age, they will understand the world differently. It's no surprise that you must talk to a toddler differently than a teenager. However, during those years in between, subtle changes are happening in your child's brain.

Your child's physical changes are easy to see. When your child goes through a physical growth spurt, they'll suddenly outgrow their clothing and eat seconds at every meal. Mental growth spurts are harder to identify, though. One day they'll want to play with baby dolls, and the next, they're telling you they want to wear makeup now. You're left wondering, *when exactly did they become aware of makeup and decide they were interested?*

In this chapter, I'll walk you through some communication examples you can use with children at different stages of their development. Keep in mind that children's brains develop at varying rates, so even if your child is in the toddler stage, for instance, they may not communicate the same way other toddlers do.

Over time, you'll learn the most effective ways to communicate with your child. Your parent-child bond will strengthen. Slowly, you'll notice your home environment changing from one filled with shouting and tears to one that's pleasant and peaceful. And who doesn't want that?

COMMUNICATION EXAMPLES FOR BABIES AND TODDLERS

Did you realize that babies, even before they become toddlers, already show signs of communication? Typically, when a baby is only three months old, they can already respond to things you say. Of course, they're not going to blurt out, "Hey Ma, how about that bottle you promised?" at this age (let's all admit this would be utterly terrifying), but they will begin to smile at you as you talk to them.

When they smile or stop crying when they hear your voice, this means that they are hearing you speak. It also means that they've developed some understanding that your voice belongs to *you*. When your voice is near, you are near. The same is true for your partner.

While most children don't begin speaking until around 12 months, they will start using vocalizations and facial expressions to get their point across. For the typical baby, cooing sounds are their attempt at imitating our speech. They also get crafty with that one key sound infants are infamous for: crying. Babies can develop different cries depending on what they want.

If you think your baby's hungry cry is different from their "I need a diaper change" cry, you are absolutely correct. Pretty cool, right?

As your baby begins to grow into a toddler, they'll start picking up on more communication skills. The toddler period is that super important time from two years old to three years old. You'll notice they seem to just absorb words left and right.

When children are two, they usually start stringing together words. They might say sentences like "Me too" or "I go!" You'll also hear every parent's favorite word many, many times: "No!" And sometimes you'll hear that word screamed out *several* times in a row ("No, no, no, no. no! No bath!"). This age is also when kids begin to develop a sense of self, and they'll start talking in the first person, using words like "I" and "me."

By their third year, most kids are starting to become little talking machines. They may know up to 200 words at this point, which is pretty remarkable, considering they've only been alive for 36 months! They can start having small conversations with you. ("Which shirt do you want?" "This shirt!")

While some aspects of communicating are genetic (for instance, a kid must be able to use certain mouth muscles to speak), parents can also nurture a child's communication abilities. This is where you can use your gentle parenting skills.

When your child is still an infant, you can start reading to them. Even reading to them from day one (yes, that day you bring them home from the hospital) can foster good communication skills. Keep reading to them as they grow older. You can talk to them often and sing kids songs. Don't worry; they're not going to judge you on your singing skills (Yet. That happens when they're a little older.).

You can play games like Simon Says. This game is great because kids learn new words (head, ear, nose, etc.) but also get introduced to directions, like "Touch your nose." They also have to listen closely to determine if you've said, "Simon Says."

Even if your child can't talk back to you yet, you can pay attention to those communication signals that show they understand. Are they smiling when they hear a word they like, such as "dog"? Are they clapping when you sing their favorite song? They might try to grab the book you're reading to look at it. They may try to repeat the words back to you with babbling sounds. These are all signs that your child is listening and starting to understand.

For children who haven't started using words, you can repeat their babbling sounds and add a few extra sounds of your own. This way, your baby will begin to understand that communication involves using similar words and creating your own.

You might be wondering why talking to your baby is important to anger management. How could singing "Mary Had a Little Lamb" over and over keep you from screaming at the top of your lungs down the road?

There are a few reasons. First, you'll bond with your child during these activities. Communicating with your child through activities that engage them is a great way to show them you care about their feelings and needs. You're also helping them develop the skills to express their feelings. This open communication can prevent conflict down the road.

When your child can express their thoughts through words or body language (like shaking their head no), they will be less likely to resort to tantrums to get what they want.

This is also a golden opportunity for teaching your child emotional regulation at a young age. When they start getting upset over something, you can catch them off guard and ask them to touch their nose. They'll instinctively follow your direction (all that Simon Says practice paid off!), and before they know it, the angry moment has passed.

COMMUNICATION EXAMPLES FOR YOUNG CHILDREN

Children fall into the "young child" category when they've outgrown the toddler years but aren't quite preteens. In other words, the term "young child" refers to a kid between four and eight years old.

This age group can be especially fun for parents because this is the age that children really begin to expand their speaking skills. They'll start to tell you stories (sometimes fantastical ones that you're certain aren't true), but this is all part of learning about the real world and exploring their imagination.

At this stage, your child will begin to express their opinions. They'll want to talk with you about their day and will look to you for approval. This period is just as crucial for fostering a bond because you'll be setting the tone of your communication style for years to come.

What are some examples of how you can communicate with a young child? When they're telling you something, use those active listening skills we talked about earlier in this book. Instead of getting caught up in whether your child uses the past tense correctly, pay attention to the information they're trying to tell you.

Show them that you're listening and not just critiquing their word choice. If they're telling you this story, it means something to them. "Oh, you made a popsicle picture frame in art class today? That sounds really creative. What sorts of colors did you use?" Having a real conversation with your child instead of just nodding absentmindedly will help them understand that their experiences are just as valid and important as yours.

Another way you can model positive communication strategies is by looking for ways to praise them. If they've put away their toys without asking, let them know you appreciate it. You'll be modeling gratitude for them, and they're more likely to give it back. One day, you might hear your child say, "Thanks for taking me to soccer practice, Dad" or "I'm glad you came to my recital, Mom."

Don't forget that communication isn't just about words! Verbal communication also involves the tone of your voice as well as the manner in which you speak (i.e., your child is much more likely to understand when you say, "That's the neighbor's dog," versus "That's the attorney's Dobermann.").

Your kid is also paying attention to your nonverbal communication skills. Remember how we talked about babies using smiles and cries to communicate? They learned a lot of that from you! Now that they're older, they're paying even closer attention to your facial expressions. They're very aware of whether you give them hugs or if you're flailing your hands around while you speak.

As the parent of a young child, you can foster great communication with your young child by:

- **Being aware of your body language.** Are you crossing your arms because you're upset? Are you rolling your eyes when they stumble on their words? Or are you maintaining eye contact with your child to show that you're respectfully listening to what they're saying?
- **Understanding your child's perspective.** If they're talking about being scared of someone in an Easter bunny costume, consider the situation through their eyes. A huge, furry rabbit fifty times the normal size is trying to hug them. You probably ran the first time you saw such a thing, too!
- **Using positive language.** Don't belittle your child when you're talking with them. Model appropriate, kind behavior when talking with them. Instead of saying, "That really was a stupid thing you did just then," help them prepare better for the situation next time. "It might be a good idea to close the milk carton before you shake it next time; what do you think?"
- **Helping them talk about their feelings.** If you, the parent, have difficulty understanding your feelings, how do you think your five-year-old feels? They've had much less time to learn about the complex nature of human emotions. Help them label their emotions. You might say things like, "Do you think you might be feeling scared because that amusement park ride is kind of high up?" or "When someone does something nice for me, it

makes me so happy. Is that how you're feeling right now?"

- **Using specific language.** When praising our child, we might find ourselves saying things like, "Nice work!" or "Good job!" While it's sometimes clear to the child what they did well, don't leave them guessing. (Did you ever spend all night writing an essay or finishing a homework assignment only to receive a checkmark from the teacher or a sticker? You wanted a little more recognition for your hard work!) Use "noticing" statements when praising them. For instance, tell them, "I noticed you asked that girl sitting by herself if she wanted to swing with you. That's awesome; you were such a great friend!"

COMMUNICATION EXAMPLES FOR PRE-TEENS

Preteens are typically considered to be from about nine to twelve. This can be a somewhat awkward stage for many kids because they're balancing that overlap of being a young child and getting ready to become a teenager. They still want to play and act goofy, but they also want to look cool in front of their friends.

As you can imagine, this is another perfect stage for strengthening your parent-child relationship. Communication begins to change in certain ways, as your child will begin to have "bigger" questions, including questions about menstruation and sex.

While you may think your child is too young to know about these topics, chances are they've already heard about them. You want to make sure they're hearing appropriate and accurate information. Show your child they can discuss these important, sometimes uncomfortable, issues with you.

You can do this by pointing out when a commercial or news story mentions sex or menstruation. You can then ask your child whether they have questions about these subjects, and let them know that they can come to you in the future for help. For instance, if a tampon commercial comes on, you can ask your daughter, "Do you know what tampons are used for?" This can help initiate the conversation.

Like children of other ages, preteens want to know they're being listened to. You can further foster good communication skills by giving them your undivided attention. When you let the phone ring instead of answering it while they're talking, you show them they're a priority. When you ask them if they want to watch a movie with you instead of jumping on your work computer after dinner, you're showing them that you value their time and presence.

Re-engaging with your child in these ways can demonstrate that you're not the angry parent you used to be. You want to connect with them on a personal level. Here are some examples of other things you can do to build a good connection with your preteen:

- **Spend some everyday moments with them.** Big bonding moments aren't always those European vacations or treehouse construction projects. Bonding happens in those smaller moments, too, such as when you cook dinners together or play a game of basketball in the backyard. These ordinary

moments are when your child may feel the most comfortable opening up to you.
- **Remain involved in your child's life.** At this age, your child is likely going to start exploring their own interests, and there's a good chance they don't want their hand held while doing so! You can still support them by rooting for them at the track meet or proudly displaying their artwork on the living room wall.
- **Consider their personality.** If your child is an introverted person, they may have a harder time talking. They may even prefer to spend time together that doesn't involve much talking. Remember, you are still communicating even when doing something like gardening together. Your child may feel more comfortable opening up in these quieter, one-on-one settings.
- **Avoid yes-or-no questions.** While this type of question isn't bad by nature, a yes-or-no question isn't very helpful when you want to invite communication with your child. If you're interested in learning more about your child's band practice session, you can ask them, "You mentioned last time the clarinet section was having a hard time keeping up with the rest of the band. How did they sound this time?"

Remember, children begin to have more pressure put on them during middle school. This is the age when they may begin to feel social pressure to look or act a certain way. Their teachers will begin to expect more from them when it comes to grades and homework assignments. Communicate with your child about the strategies you use to regulate your emotions.

Your child has seen you angry in the past, and knowing that a calming method has worked for you can be a huge incentive to try it out for themselves.

COMMUNICATION EXAMPLES FOR TEENAGERS

When your child turns thirteen, you can both celebrate. They've officially reached their teenage years! While teenagers get a bad rap for being moody and volatile, there will still be moments to bond and appreciate having reached this milestone. Your child is entering a new phase, one where they'll have many more opportunities in school and social circles. They'll begin to make plans for adulthood. It sounds impossible, but it's true. Your little one will be flying the coop soon.

But don't shed any tears just yet. You still have plenty of parenting duties before you send them off on their own. And helping your child navigate those wild teenage years is one big duty!

First, don't feel completely rejected when your child tells you nothing interesting happened at school, but you overhear them telling their best friend that there was an actual fire in math class today. Your teenager is strengthening their social bonds these days, which is a great thing!

You can still reach out to your child and be that safe place for them. Keep in mind, they may be intentionally testing your limits these days. Try to avoid passing judgment when they tell you they plan to get a large face tattoo the moment they turn eighteen. Instead, encourage discussion about why they want to get a prominent tattoo and what they're trying to convey by doing so. In a case like this, a parent might say, "That's interesting you're thinking about doing that. I'm curious what made you decide to go that route?"

Emotions can be all over the place during the teenage years. One minute your child is laughing her heart out with her bestie; the next, she's crying because she broke up with her boyfriend of two months. When your child is feeling a strong emotion, make sure you validate that feeling. Instead of saying, "Why are you sobbing over a two-month relationship? That's ridiculous," you can say, "I'm sorry to see you so sad from your breakup. Is there something that might help take your mind off it? Tonight might be a good night to try that restaurant your friends liked."

Don't be afraid to schedule time together. Just like you're now scheduling in self-care time (you are, right?!), you should schedule time to spend with your teenager. Their schedule is likely getting busier by the minute, but it's important that you find time to hang out with them. You can attend their sibling's theater performance or catch a movie together.

Active listening at this stage is crucial. Your teenager will probably be offended that you don't remember the name of every friend or teacher. While in some cases, this is impossible (especially when they know three Zoeys and four Liams), you can do your best to pay attention to their stories. Take an interest in your child's passion. Ask them about that band they are obsessed with or that new sneaker brand they've been talking about.

If your teen has a difficult time talking through their problems, consider giving them a journal (preteens may like this strategy, too!). They can write out their questions to you instead of having to say them aloud. Sometimes, saying what's on their mind can be embarrassing and awkward. When your teen is ready, they can give you the journal to read and respond to. Don't wait too long to write your response, though. Answering within a day is a good goal since you don't want your child to think you're ignoring their problem.

One of the most important things you can do now is show that you trust your child. They're very aware of the fact they'll be reaching adulthood soon, and you want to show them that you have confidence that they can handle what life throws their way. Ask them to do a favor for you that demonstrates this confidence, such as driving your new car for an oil change or making a bank deposit for you.

The teenage years are wonderful opportunities for communicating your love for your kid, even if they're growing up fast. Keeping your parent-child bond strong will help you both navigate their first years into adulthood a little easier.

COMMUNICATION WORKSHEET

Sometimes, the easiest way to express our feelings is by putting them down on paper. You can do a family exercise with the following worksheet to help everyone in your household communicate more effectively.

Pick a family member: (Example: Mom)

_____

Draw an emoji that represents how you and that person communicate. (Example: 😠 *angry face emoji*)

_____

Why did you pick that emoji? (Example: Because she's always mad at me.)

_____

What is an example of a time you and your family member represented that emoji? (Example: When I dropped the glass and it broke, making a big mess.)

_____

What do you wish your family member would have done instead? (Example: I wish she would have understood the glass was slippery, and it fell out of my hands by accident.)

_____

What emoji would you like to represent your relationship with your family member? (Example: 🤪 *zany face emoji*)

_____

Why did you pick that emoji? (Example: Because the most fun times are when we're being silly together and singing funny songs.)

What can your family member do to be more like that emoji? (Example: They can shout less and not make me sad when I make a mistake.)

You're now armed with plenty of examples you can use to navigate conversations with your child. The path looks bright ahead, doesn't it? It can stay that way if you continue with your anger management strategies. In the next chapter, we'll discuss coping skills and resiliency strategies to keep you motivated throughout parenthood so you don't resort to your old ways.

Chapter Takeaways:

- Children have different communication needs and abilities depending on their age.
- Modeling good communication skills for your child can help them learn to communicate with you and develop emotional control.
- Using active listening and other strategies with your child can strengthen your parent-child relationship.

9

BUILDING RESILIENCE AND COPING SKILLS FOR LIFE

"Resiliency is something you do, more than something you have... You become highly resilient by continuously learning your best way of being yourself in your circumstance."

— AL SIEBERT

At this point, you probably feel ready to conquer the world. You're acknowledging when you're starting to feel those first sparks of anger. That recognition of your emotions is helping you know when to disengage from a situation that could get worse. And now, you've learned some strategies for re-engaging with your child.

What more could there possibly be, you ask?

Before you pin on that SuperParent cape, there's something you should know. These strategies that you've learned have to be put into action. And sometimes, you're going to forget.

You're going to get triggered by something, and that fuse inside you is going to burn pretty darn quickly. But that's part of life. We all make mistakes.

In this chapter, I will share some ways you and your child can become resilient. Resiliency is the ability to "bounce back" after mishaps. If you're resilient, you don't let small missteps, or even bigger setbacks, ruin your day. A resilient parent admits that they made a mistake, they correct the situation, and they move on. Or if something happens to them that's out of their control, they acknowledge what's happened and use the appropriate tools to get past it.

You don't need to spend a lifetime regretting each and every mistake you make. That's not productive, and you wouldn't want your child to pick up on that ruminating behavior. Instead, we accept that mistakes happen and try to do better next time. When life throws lemons our way, we turn them into lemonade.

STRATEGIES FOR BUILDING RESILIENCE IN PARENTS AND CHILDREN

Before you started managing your anger, your child (and your partner) likely didn't know what to expect from you. The only constant in your relationship with them may have been that they knew you were going to get angry, but they weren't exactly sure *in which way* you were going to get mad.

Don't throw your family back into that cycle of unpredictability. Work on your resiliency so that you can maintain a peaceful and consistent home environment, even in the face of trauma and adversity.

Nobody wants to slip into their old anger patterns, but it can be hard not to when we're faced with unexpected life changes. For example, imagine that you've worked really hard to manage your work stress so that you're not bringing it home to your child each day. But suddenly, you get laid off and have to find a new job. All that previous work stress has come back three-fold. It suddenly seems easier to get worked up over those small things your child does.

Some other things that may lead you back down the wrong path are:

- A disaster (your house catches on fire or is flooded)
- Substance abuse (you start experiencing problems with alcohol or drugs)
- A relationship falls through (you get divorced or break up with a long-term partner)
- A family member passes away (or gets seriously ill)

In these instances, it's often not the event itself (such as the fire or the divorce) that causes problems for children. Interestingly, it's how the child's parent deals with those events. In other words, if you and your child's father separate, you may be worried your kid will experience long-term issues from the parents living in different homes. However, the real problems will start to form when your child listens to you bad-mouth their father or get into heated arguments with him every time you drop them off.

Thankfully, strengthening your resiliency can keep you on the right path. The everyday things we do to practice self-care look a lot like building resiliency. In fact, a traumatic event is a fitting opportunity to assess our current strategies for dealing with problems.

Some things you can do to build resilience for yourself include:

- **Keep a log of the self-care activities you are doing for yourself.** Sometimes, seeing the list in writing will help you get an accurate idea of what it is you're doing and not doing. For example, you may say, "Oh, I'm getting to the gym for a workout fairly regularly to help manage my stress." Yet when you look back at your log, you may realize you've only gone twice in the past month. This information can be a wake-up call that you need to devote more time to self-care.
- **Get in touch with others.** When you're dealing with a sudden event like a family member passing away, you will be busy handling all sorts of affairs like funeral arrangements and financial concerns. It's easy to become isolated from others when you're in the midst of grief and sifting through the mountain of belongings your loved one left behind. Reach out to others and ask for help with these tasks. Friends and family are there for you.
- **Put the problem in perspective.** In the moment of a major problem, it's easy to assume we will live in chaos for the rest of our lives. But putting the issue in perspective can help you get a healthy, rational view.
- **Journal out the experience.** Writing out those feelings bubbling up inside you can be incredibly cleansing for your soul. If you don't feel like talking

about your problems with someone, journaling is a good, private way to get those emotions out. You can always lock up your diary or burn your writing if you feel too vulnerable afterward.

- **Volunteer to help someone in a similar situation.** If you've just gone through cancer treatment, consider supporting someone who has just been diagnosed. Helping someone else through a difficult time can make us feel empowered.

Let's look at a scenario where a parent has an opportunity to be resilient.

Imagine you've been involved in a car accident and broken your arm. Your car is completely totaled, and insurance isn't going to pay for it. In this case, you're going to feel pretty shoddy for a few months. That's normal.

You may be stressed thinking you'll never recover from the financial hit of replacing the car. You may also feel like you're going to fall behind at work since you can't type as fast with the injured arm.

However, you put your self-care and resiliency strategies into practice during this time. With a clear, focused mind, you realize you can save up for a down payment on a new car quickly since you're no longer paying for car insurance, gas money, or auto repairs. You remember hearing about a voice-recognition software program that converts words to text. You install this program on your computer so that it types what you dictate, and it ends up helping you work even faster than before your accident.

With time, you realize you've overcome what was a potentially life-altering problem. You were able to keep your cool and maintain a positive, healthy relationship with your child.

But you're not the only one you need to worry about when your family faces adversity. Children pick up on more than you can imagine, and it's essential that they learn resiliency strategies, too. Luckily, many of the things you do to keep your mind and body healthy will work for your child!

Children thrive on routines. When they get up at the same time, eat lunch at the same time, and go to bed at the same time, they feel safe. They know what to expect each day. If your family has been thrown into chaos by relocating to a new city, keep up what routines you can. This will provide a sense of normalcy that can help everyone feel a little more at ease.

Like adults, children love helping others. The same child who has relocated may want to help younger kids at school who have also just moved to the area. Speak with your child's teacher to see if they might be able to mentor this younger child and help them adjust.

Remember that you can help your child connect with others. If your kid has been through a traumatic situation, such as losing a close family member, consider enrolling them in a support group of their peers. Hearing children their age talk about their feelings can encourage your child to process their own grief.

Help your child practice gratitude. In the face of adversity, it's easy to focus on the terrible things that have happened to us. Remind your child of all the great things that are present in their life. Ask them to tell you about the people and experiences they're grateful for. They can even write these thoughts down in a journal each evening before bedtime.

Just like you, your child will be less likely to resort to angry outbursts to vent their stress if given the appropriate tools. While no family wants to deal with trauma, you can do everything in your power to ensure you're all working on creating a stable, calm home environment.

MAINTAINING PROGRESS AND LONG-TERM ANGER MANAGEMENT

Some parents experience the occasional angry episode, while others exhibit chronic anger. Anger is considered chronic when it doesn't go away after time passes and begins to dominate a person's thoughts and actions. This, unfortunately, means you spend a lot of your day thinking about your anger and acting on it.

You could have chronic anger if you notice that you get into arguments with many different people. For instance, you may find that your child isn't the only target of your anger but that you also get into disagreements with coworkers, siblings, and even strangers. Other signs of chronic anger include being physically or verbally abusive to others and getting so mad that you say things you regret.

Chronic anger has a lot of causes which can include past trauma, genetics, medical conditions, and environmental factors. No matter what has caused a person's chronic anger, there are options for managing it. And when you manage it effectively, you can get long-term results.

Parents with chronic anger may have more trouble managing their anger because they are used to reacting angrily throughout much of the day. Online therapy has been found to be especially effective in helping people with this condition. Making lifestyle changes may also be necessary to avoid some of the most common triggers. While certain changes like switching jobs or partners can seem difficult or nearly impossible, the change may ultimately increase your quality of life and, subsequently, your child's quality of life.

Once you begin consistently managing your anger, your self-esteem will also improve. No parent wants to feel like they're the mean mommy or daddy, and overcoming the shame associated with our anger can take time. Give yourself a chance, though!

Recognize your successes. Remember, you're not just managing your anger for your mental health but your physical health, too.

STAYING MOTIVATED AND AVOIDING RELAPSE

I'm not going to lie. The going will get tough sometimes. There will be days when you've just spent hours cleaning the house from top to bottom before the in-laws stop by, and your child runs through the house with muddy sneakers. There will be other times when you'll find out that your child got into a fight on the playground and pushed another kid.

These are moments that can threaten a "relapse." Relapse comes in three stages, including emotional, mental, and physical relapses. Emotional relapse is when you start keeping those emotions in. Instead of dealing with that rising anger, you just let it build. Mental relapse is when you think about how easy it would be to let yourself let all that anger out right now.

You start telling yourself that you don't need to disengage from the situation. You might even pretend you're not feeling angry. Physical relapse is when you let yourself slip into those old habits, yell uncontrollably, and fly into a fit of rage.

Try to nip temptation in the bud. When you start to feel angry, remember that it's okay to acknowledge it. In fact, you should! It's a healthy thing to do. Think back to all those times when you tried to pretend you weren't angry. Didn't work, did it?

Be persistent when it comes to disengaging from the situation. If your child is trying to push your buttons, take a step back. Remember to communicate that you are going to take a moment for yourself. Pull on those calming strategies. Count to 10. Meditate or listen to music for a few minutes. Refer to your calm-down box. Whatever it takes, do it.

You can even consider making a contact list of people you can call when you feel like you're at your wit's end. Whip out this list when you feel that anger get to you. The people you call might be friends, family members, religious leaders, or even people you've met in anger management support groups.

Once you've managed to rein in your anger, you can then re-engage with your child. Refer back to those communication strategies we covered in the last chapter. Communicate with your child clearly about what went wrong. If you said or did something that you shouldn't have, apologize. Make amends, and come up with a solution together.

Relationships are a continuous process. They take work on both ends. Both you and your child are responsible for learning to regulate your emotions. Like other humans, you will each say things you regret from time to time. The important thing is that you communicate and fall back on that strong parent-child bond you've spent so much time working on.

RESILIENCY WORKSHEET

When you've managed to handle a situation well, give yourself a pat on the back! You've been working hard on your anger management skills, and that work is paying off. However, anger management is an ongoing process, especially if you're dealing with chronic anger. This worksheet lists journal prompts you can use to periodically reflect on your resiliency levels.

What is a situation that made you angry recently? How did you handle the situation, and was it healthy, in hindsight? If not, what could you do differently next time? (Example: My child made me mad when they opened the car door onto a stranger's car in the parking lot. I yelled at them and asked why they hadn't listened to me when I said to be careful. I'm not proud of how I handled the situation because my daughter's feelings were hurt, and the driver of the other car looked uncomfortable. Next time, I will open the car door for my child so I can protect the other car. If she accidentally does it again, I will take a ten-second breather and acknowledge it was an accident.)

What are you currently stressed about? What are you doing to manage your stress levels? (Example: I'm stressed because my boss expects me to stay late at the office every day. I'm trying to eliminate this stress by telling him I can stay late twice a week, but I need to be home on time the other three days. In the meantime, I'm doing a quick yoga session each morning and making sure I take my full lunch break.)

What is your biggest challenge to doing self-care? What can be done about this?

(Example: My schedule is really packed these days between work and the kids' extracurriculars. I'm going to ask one of the other parents if they'd be willing to switch carpool duty so we can each have a day or two off each week. I'll use this time for self-care.)

Who are your biggest supporters when it comes to helping you be resilient?

(Example: My child and partner have both been cheering me on since I told them I'm working on my anger management. My sister is also a big support because she's offered to be my go-to contact person when I need to step away from a situation.)

Chapter Takeaways:

- Resilient parents are ones who keep going even when faced with tough circumstances.
- Anger management is a continuous process. Mistakes happen, and that's okay.
- Using a combination of resiliency and self-care strategies can keep anger at bay and foster a healthy home environment.

Now that you've reached the end of the book, you might be feeling a little unsure of what comes next. The truth is, there are many unknowns out there. You don't know if your child will come home with a negative report from their teacher or if they'll refuse to eat dinner tonight.

But you also don't know if your kid will hit that home run during the baseball game or get an A+ on that book report.

What you do know is that you love your child, and no matter what situation comes your way, you're going to do your best to respond appropriately and demonstrate that love.

THE EASY WAY TO HELP ANOTHER FAMILY

We all want the best for our children, and working on ourselves is one of the most effective ways of ensuring it. Take this opportunity to share the wisdom with other parents.

Simply by sharing your honest opinion of this book and a little about your own story, you'll show new readers that they're not alone – and you'll point them in the direction of exactly the resource they need to make a change.

IN UNDER 1 MINUTE
YOU CAN HELP OTHERS JUST LIKE YOU BY LEAVING A REVIEW!

Thank you so much for your support. It has more of an impact than you realize.

Scan the QR code to leave a review!

CONCLUSION

You've probably heard the saying, "It's the journey, not the destination." When it comes to anger management, this couldn't be more true. You've embarked on an amazing journey for yourself and your child, and along the way, you will find more strength and resiliency than you ever thought possible.

If you haven't already, show a little gratitude to yourself for being brave and picking up this book. I know it wasn't easy. No one likes to admit that they've been doing things the wrong way, especially when we're parents. It takes even greater strength to come to terms with this fact and then actively seek ways to repair the damage.

There are no quick solutions for eliminating anger from your life, unfortunately. As we've discussed in this book, my three-step process is a guide for managing your anger, but it's not a magic tool to armor yourself against anger. In other words, anger is inevitable.

Sometimes, anger can even be healthy. When we get mad that we got a low score on a test, this anger can motivate us to perform better. When we get upset that our coworker got a raise and we didn't, our anger can light a fire under us to finally ask our boss for a higher salary. If we shout when our child is about to run into traffic, this yelling alerts them to watch out for that car.

But uncontrolled rage is never good. It's not good for your body because it raises your blood pressure. If you experience prolonged high blood pressure, you could be more at risk for heart disease and even a heart attack. You'll feel physically exhausted if you allow anger to constantly overtake your body.

Mentally, being angry all the time feels terrible. And most importantly, constant, recurring anger can destroy your relationship with your child. It can cause your child to withdraw from you. They'll feel nervous around you, fearing they'll make mistakes. It will come as no surprise then that your child won't feel comfortable coming to you in times of need.

You can let out that breath you've been holding throughout your parenting days. You've got some tools now! You've put in the effort to read this book, and you've (hopefully) come away with some practical strategies that will help you repair and strengthen your relationship with your kid.

You've learned to:

- **Acknowledge your anger.** You've learned about fear-based, passive-aggressive, pain-based, and explosive anger. Putting a name to your emotions is a key step to managing them appropriately.

We've also discussed gentle parenting, an approach that can help you put your anger aside and focus on your child's needs first. Additionally, you've learned some ways that you can avoid parental triggers and minimize conflict.

- **Disengage from the situation.** Acting in the moment is rarely a good thing. Instead of correcting your child in the moment, step away from the situation for a moment. Acknowledge that you're angry, and then use the strategy of your choice to calm yourself down (such as deep breathing or mindfulness).

You can incorporate yoga and other exercise into your daily routine as a way to channel some of your anger into good feelings. You can also create a calm-down box that is filled with objects that remind you of peace and tranquility.

- **Re-engage with your child.** When you are in the right headspace, you can communicate with your child in a loving way. Discuss what happened. Make apologies if necessary. Include your child in the problem-solving process. Ask for their input so that they can feel like they're part of the solution.

Keep in mind that life loves to throw us curveballs. Just when you think you're coasting for the rest of your parenting years, you will surely hit a bump in the road. These can't be prevented. What you can prevent, however, is reacting angrily. Focus on being a resilient parent and get through those challenges using the strategies you've learned.

Congratulations on reaching this milestone! You've worked hard to get to this point. Now, go for a run to let off some steam, meditate, and reflect on what you've learned, or turn to your gratitude journal and write down how thankful you are for having the courage to overcome your anger!

Your child will be much better off with a parent who loves them enough to work on themselves. No one is perfect. I'm not, you aren't, and neither is your child. But your relationship with your child can be perfect if you continue to dedicate time and energy to taking responsibility for your anger.

I wish you the best of luck in your journey!

If you've found this book helpful, please leave a review. Your rating can help another parent find the tools to rebuild a relationship with their own child!

REFERENCES

American Psychological Association. (2011, October 1). *Strategies for controlling your anger: Keeping anger in check*. https://www.apa.org. https://www.apa.org/topics/anger/strategies-controlling

American Psychological Association. (2012). *Resilience guide for parents and teachers*. https://www.apa.org/topics/resilience/guide-parents-teachers

American Psychological Association. (2017, August 17). *Positive discipline by age*. https://www.apa.org. https://www.apa.org/act/resources/fact-sheets/positive-discipline

Anger management quotes. (n.d.). Goodreads. Retrieved July 23, 2023, from https://www.goodreads.com/quotes/tag/anger-management

Anger Quotes. (n.d.). https://bookroo.com/quotes/anger

Anger - how it affects people. (n.d.). Better Health Channel. https://www.betterhealth.vic.gov.au/health/healthyliving/anger-how-it-affects-people

Bad parenting quotes (19 quotes). (n.d.). Goodreads. Retrieved July 23, 2023, from https://www.goodreads.com/quotes/tag/bad-parenting

Bean, S. (2022, May 18). *How to walk away from a fight with your child*. Empowering Parents. https://www.empoweringparents.com/article/how-to-walk-away-from-a-fight-with-your-child/

Berttucci, A. (2018). *How to reconnect with your kids after conflict* [VIDEO]. Cedar Tree Counseling. https://cedartreecounseling.com/blog/how-to-reconnect-with-your-kids-after-conflict/

BetterHelp. (2023, April 26). *What chronic anger is and how to manage it*. Retrieved July 24, 2023, from https://www.betterhelp.com/advice/anger/what-chronic-anger-is-and-how-to-manage-it/

Between parent and child quotes by Haim G. Ginott. (n.d.). Retrieved July 23, 2023, from https://www.goodreads.com/work/quotes/248119-between-parent-and-child[CK1] [CP2]

Black, B. (2010, March 15). *The link between anger and stress*. MentalHelp.net. Retrieved July 23, 2023, from https://www.mentalhelp.net/blogs/the-link-between-anger-and-stress/

Ceder, J. (2023). *Mindful parenting: How to respond instead of react*. The Gottman Institute. https://www.gottman.com/blog/mindful-parent

ing-how-to-respond-instead-of-react/#:~:text=to%20be%20present.-,Mindful%20parenting%20means%20that%20you%20bring%20your%20conscious%20attention%20to,change%20it%20or%20ignore%20it

Chowdhury, M. R. (2019). *Emotional regulation: 6 key skills to regulate emotions.* PositivePsychology.com. https://positivepsychology.com/emotion-regulation

Citizen Advocates. (2021). *When relapse threatens—what you can do to prevent it.* Citizen Advocates. https://citizenadvocates.net/blog/when-relapse-threatens-what-you-can-do-to-prevent-it/

Clarke University. (2017, January 9). Tips for managing conflict. https://www.clarke.edu/campus-life/health-wellness/counseling/articles-advice/tips-for-managing-conflict/[CK3] [CP4]

Clarke-Fields, H. (2020, March 7). *A parenting expert shares the common mistake that psychologically damages kids—and what to do instead.* CNBC. https://www.cnbc.com/2019/12/11/the-common-yet-parenting-mistake-that-psychologically-damages-kids-according-to-expert.html

Communication & anger. (n.d.). Tutorialspoint. Retrieved July 23, 2023, from https://www.tutorialspoint.com/anger_management/communication_and_anger.htm

Communication and your 2- to 3-year-old. (2022, May). Nemours KidsHealth[CK5] . Retrieved July 23, 2023, from https://kidshealth.org/en/parents/comm-2-to-3.html

Connecting with your preteen. (2022b, July). Nemours KidsHealth. Retrieved July 24, 2023, from https://kidshealth.org/en/parents/preteen.html

Conte, C. (2017, March 15). *5 quick tips for handling the anger you have toward family.* Dr. Christian Conte. Retrieved July 23, 2023, from https://www.drchristianconte.com/5-quick-tips-handling-anger-toward-family/

Controlling your anger as a parent. (2021, August). Pregnancy Birth and Baby. https://www.pregnancybirthbaby.org.au/controlling-your-anger-as-a-parent

Dacy, A. (n.d.). *Communicating with baby: Tips and milestones from birth to age 5.* National Association for the Education of Young Children. Retrieved July 23, 2023, from https://www.naeyc.org/our-work/families/communicating-with-baby#:~:text=Listen%20and%20respond%20to%20your,%2Dand%2Dforth%20conversation%20skills

Daino, J. E. (2022). *How to set family boundaries: A therapist's guide.* Talkspace. https://www.talkspace.com/blog/family-boundaries/

Ehmke, R. (2023). *Tips for communicating with your teen.* Child Mind

REFERENCES | 155

Institute. https://childmind.org/article/tips-communicating-with-teen/

Erieau, C. (2020, August 17). *55 best stress quotes*. Driven. https://home.hellodriven.com/articles/55-best-stress-quotes/

Exchange Family Center. (2017). *Protective factors: Meet parenting stress with parental resilience*. Exchange Family Center. https://www.exchangefamilycenter.org/exchange-family-center-blog/2017/12/14/protective-factors-meet-parenting-stress-with-parental-resilience

Family conflict. (n.d.). Better Health Channel. Retrieved July 23, 2023, from https://www.betterhealth.vic.gov.au/health/healthyliving/family-conflict

Flatley, K. (2021). *48 inspiring positive parenting quotes on raising kids and being a better parent*. Self-Sufficient Kids. https://selfsufficientkids.com/inspiring-positive-parenting-quotes/

Gagnon, D. (n.d.). *Do you recognize the 10 types of anger?* Montreal CBT Psychologist. Retrieved June 30, 2023, from https://www.montrealcbtpsychologist.com/blog/122622-do-you-recognize-the-10-types-of-anger_8

Gilbert, A. (2018). *Three tips to create a resilient mindset*. Center for Parent and Teen Communication. https://parentandteen.com/three-tips-resilient-mindset/

Gilles, G. (2014, May 22). *7 tips for effective communication with your school-aged child*. MentalHelp.net. Retrieved July 23, 2023, from https://www.mentalhelp.net/blogs/7-tips-for-effective-communication-with-your-school-aged-child/

Gowmon, V. (2021, June 16). *Inspiring quotes on child learning and development*. Retrieved July 23, 2023, from https://www.vincegowmon.com/inspiring-quotes-on-child-learning-and-development/

Harvey, B. E. (2018, October 23). *Effective versus ineffective parenting: Know the difference?* The Center for Parenting Education. https://centerforparentingeducation.org/library-of-articles/focus-parents/effective-versus-ineffective-parenting-know-the-difference/#:~:text=Ineffective%20parents%2C%20failing%20to%20recognize,do%20is%20an%20effective%20tool

Headspace. (n.d.). *What is mindful parenting?* Retrieved July 23, 2023, from https://www.headspace.com/mindfulness/mindful-parenting#:~:text=One%20study%20found%20that%20parents,%2C%20depression%2C%20and%20acting%20out

Hill, P. (2019, December 19). *Four things a parent must never do when angry*.

Medium. https://medium.com/a-parent-is-born/four-things-a-parent-must-never-do-when-angry-a0bfb15c9dce

Holmes, K. (2023). *10 miracle phrases to help you reconnect with your child.* Happy You, Happy Family. https://happyyouhappyfamily.com/how-to-reconnect-with-your-child/

Holmes, M. (2020, May 23). *It's okay to let your child know you're angry.* Lifestart Foundation. Retrieved July 23, 2023, from https://www.lifestartfoundation.org/parenting-tips/its-okay-to-let-your-child-know-youre-angry#:~:text=It's%20what%20you%20do%20with,fear%2C%20excitement%20and%20so%20on

Impact Factory. (2023, June 23). *Assertive communication - an anger management technique.* Retrieved July 23, 2023, from https://www.impactfactory.com/resources/assertive-communication-an-anger-management-technique/#:~:text=Good%20communication%20skills%20are%20an,how%20we%20feel%20toward%20them

Jordan, B. (2022, September 16). *4 simple mindfulness strategies to refocus and recenter when you are feeling uncreative and overwhelmed.* The Algernon Sydney Sullivan Foundation. https://sullivanfdn.org/4-simple-mindfulness-strategies-to-refocus-and-recenter-when-you-are-feeling-uncreative-and-overwhelmed/

Kadane, L. (2023). *10 proven ways to finally stop yelling at your kids.* Today's Parent. https://www.todaysparent.com/family/discipline/proven-ways-to-finally-stop-yelling-at-your-kids/

Kirby, S. (2023). *Insightful anger quotes to learn from.* Everyday Power. https://everydaypower.com/anger-quotes/

Kleimo, C. (2020). *Lost your cool with your child? Here are 5 easy steps to reconnect.* Motherly. https://www.mother.ly/parenting/how-to-apologize-after-yelling-at-your-child/

Klynn, B. (2021, June 22). *Emotional regulation: Skills, exercises, and strategies.* BetterUp. https://www.betterup.com/blog/emotional-regulation-skills

Lapsed_Lullaby. (2023, April). *This is gonna sound very basic and trivial but CRY your heart out, provide yourself triggers to cry, try all* [Comment on the online forum post *how do you re-center yourself?*]. Reddit. https://www.reddit.com/r/Meditation/comments/12shtny/how_do_you_recenter_yourself/

Li, P. (2023). *4 types of parenting styles and their effects on children.* Parenting for Brain. https://www.parentingforbrain.com/4-baumrind-parenting-styles/

Markham, L. (2016). *How to handle your anger at your child.* Psychology

Today. https://www.psychologytoday.com/us/blog/peaceful-parents-happy-kids/201605/how-handle-your-anger-your-child

Mele, M. (2020). *Pranayama practice: Adham pranayama*. Five Prana. https://www.fiveprana.com/blog/adham-pranayama

middleearthnj. (2019, December 9). How to get a teen to talk about their feelings? Middle Earth. Retrieved July 24, 2023, from https://middleearthnj.org/2019/12/09/how-to-get-a-teen-to-talk-about-their-feelings/

Miller, C. (2023). *How to handle tantrums and meltdowns*. Child Mind Institute. https://childmind.org/article/how-to-handle-tantrums-and-meltdowns/

MindTools. (n.d.). *Centering*. Retrieved July 23, 2023, from https://www.mindtools.com/ashwpqm/centering

Minkin, R., & Horowitz, J. M. (2023, January 24). *Parenting in America today*. Pew Research Center. https://www.pewresearch.org/social-trends/2023/01/24/parenting-in-america-today/

Morgan, P. (2023). *Dozens of famous and powerful resilience quotes*. Solutions for Resilience. https://www.solutionsforresilience.com/resilience-quotes/

Morin, A. (2022). *11 anger management strategies to help you calm down*. Verywell Mind. https://www.verywellmind.com/anger-management-strategies-4178870

National Domestic Violence Hotline. (n.d.). *How to cool off when angry*. The Hotline. Retrieved July 4, 2023, from https://www.thehotline.org/resources/how-to-cool-off-when-angry/

Mindfulness for your health: The benefits of living moment by moment. (2022, July 15). *NIH News in Health, June 2021*. Retrieved July 23, 2023, from https://newsinhealth.nih.gov/2021/06/mindfulness-your-health#:~:text=Studies%20suggest%20that%20focusing%20on,help%20people%20cope%20with%20pain

National Society for the Prevention of Cruelty to Children. (n.d.). *Keeping your cool*. Retrieved July 23, 2023, from https://www.moodcafe.co.uk/media/19831/keepingyourcool_wdf48060.pdf

Parentandteen.com. (2020, March 4). *Three ways to boost your resilience as a parent*. Greater Good Magazine. https://greatergood.berkeley.edu/article/item/three_ways_to_boost_your_resilience_as_a_parent

Phillips, V. (2022, January 25). *Why being a present parent is more important than perfect*. Parent Influence. https://parentinfluence.com/why-being-a-present-parent-is-more-important-than-perfect/

Pincus, D. (2021, May 26). *Parental roles: How to set healthy boundaries with your child*. Empowering Parents. https://www.empoweringparents.com/article/parental-roles-how-to-set-healthy-boundaries-with-your-child/

Pinsker, J. (2018, November 6). *Spanking is still really common and still really bad for kids*. The Atlantic. https://www.theatlantic.com/family/archive/2018/11/spanking-kids-effective/574978/

Plant, R. (2022). *Benefits and challenges of gentle parenting*. Verywell Family. https://www.verywellfamily.com/what-is-gentle-parenting-5189566#:~:text=Gentle%20parenting%20is%20an%20evidence,compassionate%20and%20enforcing%20consistent%20boundaries.s://www.thepragmaticparent.com/discipline-kids-without-yelling/

Prasad, S. (2021). *Positive words for kids*. Osmo from BYJU'S. https://www.playosmo.com/kids-learning/positive-words-for-kids/

Princeton University. (2023). *Understanding your communication style*. UMatter. Retrieved July 23, 2023, from https://umatter.princeton.edu/respect/tools/communication-styles

Priory. (2023). *Mental health and self-care: What is it and how can you practise it?* Retrieved July 23, 2023, from https://www.priorygroup.com/blog/mental-health-and-self-care

Ream, A. (2022). *When you've lost it on your kids: 5 ways to repair*. Psyched Mommy. https://www.psychedmommy.com/blog/repairing-with-your-kids

Reed, S. (2021). *15 inspiring parenting quotes to live by*. Care. https://www.care.com/c/inspirational-parenting-quotes/

Ringer, J. (2017, February 28). *Coaching corner: 4 centering practices to increase confidence and focus*. Retrieved July 23, 2023, from https://www.judyringer.com/blog/coaching-corner-4-centering-practices-to-increase-confidence-and-focus-20170228#:~:text=Physical%20exercise%2C%20yoga%2C%20deep%20breathing,practices%20to%20begin%20your%20day

Rogers, B. (2023, July 6). *Her brain doesn't know how to process anger at this age. When she's upset ask her to touch her nose* [Comment on the online forum post *My daughter just turned two and a half*.]. Facebook. https://www.facebook.com/groups/804310739715396/posts/327762537905574/?comment_id=3277640882382357

Scott, E. (2020, September 17). *How to manage anger and stress*. Verywell Mind. Retrieved July 23, 2023, from https://www.verywellmind.com/the-effects-of-anger-and-stress-3145076

Scott, E. (2023). *5 self-care practices for every area of your life*. Verywell Mind.

REFERENCES | 159

https://www.verywellmind.com/self-care-strategies-overall-stress-reduction-3144729

Self-care tips. (2020). Therapist Aid. Retrieved July 23, 2023, from https://www.therapistaid.com/worksheets/self-care-tips

Shakeshaft, J. (2012, October 8). *6 breathing exercises to relax in 10 minutes or less.* TIME. https://healthland.time.com/2012/10/08/6-breathing-exercises-to-relax-in-10-minutes-or-less/

Shapiro, J. (2020, June 5). *The life and times of Okada Torajiro and his seiza method of self-harmonization.* Kyoto Journal. Retrieved July 23, 2023, from https://www.kyotojournal.org/spirit/the-life-and-times-of-okada-torajiro-and-his-seiza-method-of-self-harmonization/

Solace Asia. (2016). *Is mindfulness a religious or spiritual practice?* Solace. https://www.solaceasia.org/blog/is-mindfulness-a-religious-or-spiritual-practice

Sommerfeldt, S. (2019). *Tips to finding your center.* Loving Roots Project. https://www.lovingrootsproject.com/allblogposts/tips-to-finding-your-center

Spehar, C. (2019, October 19). *Communication for kids worksheets.* Pinterest. Retrieved July 24, 2023, from https://www.pinterest.ph/pin/615515474057303542/

St Peter's Preparatory School. (2022, May 8). *The benefits of positive reinforcement for children.* https://stpetersprep.co.uk/news/benefits-positive-reinforcement/#:~:text=Praising%20the%20behaviour%20over%20the,are%20often%20difficult%20to%20change

Strong, D. (2015, May 29). *7 ways anger is ruining your health.* EverydayHealth. https://www.everydayhealth.com/news/ways-anger-ruining-your-health/

Sutter Health. (2019, October). *Tips and advice for talking with preteens.* Retrieved July 24, 2023, from https://www.sutterhealth.org/health/parenting-preteens-teens/emotions-mental/talking-with-preteens

Sutton, J. (2016). *Active listening: The art of empathetic conversation.* PositivePsychology.com. https://positivepsychology.com/active-listening/#google_vignette[CK6]

United Nations International Children's Emergency Fund. (n.d.-a). *11 tips for communicating with your teen.* UNICEF Parenting. Retrieved July 24, 2023, from https://www.unicef.org/parenting/child-care/11-tips-communicating-your-teen

UNICEF[CK7] [CP8] . (n.d.-b). *How to communicate effectively with your young child.* UNICEF Parenting. Retrieved July 23, 2023, from https://

www.unicef.org/parenting/child-care/9-tips-for-better-communication

United States Department of Education, United States Department of Health & Human Services, & Too Small to Fail. (2017, May 8). *Talk, read and sing together every day! Tips for preschool teachers & other early childhood education program providers.* Office of Early Childhood Development: An Office of the Administration for Children & Families. Retrieved July 23, 2023, from https://www2.ed.gov/documents/early-learning/talk-read-sing/preschool-en.pdf

University of California, Berkeley. (n.d.). *Understanding anger: The emotional and physical effects of anger.* Berkeley University Health Services. Retrieved July 9, 2023, from https://uhs.berkeley.edu/sites/default/files/understanding_anger_0.pdf

Uono, S., & Hietanen, J. K. (2015). Eye contact perception in the West and East: A cross-cultural study. *PLOS ONE, 10*(2), Article e0118094. https://doi.org/10.1371/journal.pone.0118094

Vanbuskirk, S. (2022a). *How to discipline your child in public.* Verywell Family. https://www.verywellfamily.com/how-to-manage-your-childs-behavior-at-the-grocery-store-1094860

Vanbuskirk, S. (2022b, December 12). *Teen discipline: Strategies and challenges.* Verywell Family. https://www.verywellfamily.com/discipline-strategies-for-teens-1094840

Von Flotow, J. (2015, January 20). *Is active listening possible when you're upset or angry?* Kaizen Leadership Institute. Retrieved July 23, 2023, from https://www.kaizenleadershipinstitute.com/active-listening-possible-youre-upset-angry/

Walter, J. (2021). *Mindfulness: 6 techniques to recenter yourself amid absolute chaos.* Inverse. https://www.inverse.com/mind-body/recenter-yourself-amid-chaos/amp

Weingart, P. D. (2022). *Being right or being happy: The consequences of anger in your relationship.* Goodman Psychologist Associates. https://goodmanpsych.com/the-consequences-of-anger-in-relationships/

WFMC Health. (2023, January 17). *Benefits of anger management.* Retrieved July 24, 2023, from https://wfmchealth.org/family-health-care/benefits-of-anger-management/#:~:text=There%20are%20many%20benefits%20to%20managing%20your%20anger%2C%20such%20as,a%20happy%20and%20successful%20life

Wilson, M. (2020, June 19). *22 times celebrities shared their parenting tips.* Insider. https://www.insider.com/favorite-celebrities-parenting-tips-advice-raising-kids#blake-lively-loves-the-idea-of-putting-a-comment-box-in-the-house-for-her-children-to-leave-constructive-criticism-14

Wojcicki, E. (2019, May 13). *I raised 2 successful CEOs and a doctor—here's one of the biggest mistakes I see parents making.* CNBC. https://www.cnbc.com/2019/05/08/i-raised-2-successful-ceos-and-a-doctor-here-is-one-if-the-biggest-mistakes-parents-make.html

Young children and communication. (2012, July 31). Better Health Channel. Retrieved July 23, 2023, from https://www.betterhealth.vic.gov.au/health/healthyliving/young-children-and-communication

Printed in Great Britain
by Amazon